THE HISTORY OF WOMEN IN THE MARINES

WOMEN'S FIRSTS IN THE MARINES

SAVANNAH HARRIS

© Copyright 2021 - All rights reserved.

The content contained within this book may not be reproduced, duplicated or transmitted without direct written permission from the author or the publisher.

Under no circumstances will any blame or legal responsibility be held against the publisher, or author, for any damages, reparation, or monetary loss due to the information contained within this book, either directly or indirectly.

Legal Notice:

This book is copyright protected. It is only for personal use. You cannot amend, distribute, sell, use, quote or paraphrase any part, or the content within this book, without the consent of the author or publisher.

Disclaimer Notice:

Please note the information contained within this document is for educational and entertainment purposes only. All effort has been executed to present accurate, up to date, reliable, complete information. No warranties of any kind are declared or implied. Readers acknowledge that the author is not engaged in the rendering of legal, financial, medical or professional advice. The content within this book has been derived from various sources. Please consult a licensed professional before attempting any techniques outlined in this book.

By reading this document, the reader agrees that under no circumstances is the author responsible for any losses, direct or indirect, that are incurred as a result of the use of the information contained within this document, including, but not limited to, errors, omissions, or inaccuracies.

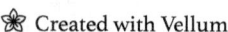 Created with Vellum

PREFACE

The history of women in the marines is fascinating and I am sure you will love this book, but it doesn't end there.

As you go through the book I challenge and invite you to think of ways you can continue this lasting legacy in your own life and extend the sisterhood to those that follow.

The last chapter includes a link to a collection of resources and information to thrive and survive.

INTRODUCTION

You can't talk about the United States Marine recruitment process without talking about "The Crucible." If you've never heard of "The Crucible," it's the final test all recruits must pass before they become a United States Marine—and it's arguably the most exhaustive. "The Crucible" is one of the most challenging tests Marine recruits must undergo, in one last, fierce push to meet their highest physical and psychological limits, stare them in the face, and win. The final challenge has put prospective Marines through a grueling 54-hour event since 1996; and it's a notorious feat.

During "The Crucible," platoons are split into squads. A drill instructor leads each squad, and each recruit in the squad takes a turn as the leader. Despite the typical boot camp routine of eight hours of sleep and three meals per day, "The Crucible" only allows recruits six hours of sleep and three meals, ready-to-eat (MREs) in the 54-hour period (Grove, 2018). The sheer lack of sleep is enough to test any person's mettle, but those who make it through become official members of the U.S. Marine Corps.

A Crucible held for recruits from the U.S. Marine Corps Recruit Depot San Diego, Lima Company in April 2021 was a history-making feat for 53 women. The 53 female recruits became the first-ever to participate in the Crucible on the West Coast, working in their all-female Platoon 3241, which was mixed with Lima Company's five other all-male platoons.

These 53 women camped outdoors, received only three hours of sleep per night, and participated in a 9-mile (15-kilometers) hike alongside the men, carrying rifles and 50-pound (23-kilogram) backpacks. They fought their way up the final hill, screaming at the last leg of their trip, the sight of the Pacific Ocean a sign that they'd prevailed. During this Crucible, these female recruits took part in a mock-village scenario under fire from simulated machine gunfire and explosions. As they fought to see through the dust, the female recruits carried the men on their shoulders. After lifting comrades, they sparred with other recruits in cages and endured a grueling obstacle course.

Before the female platoon's success at Camp Pendleton, female recruits and drill instructors could only graduate from the Marine boot camp at Parris Island, South Carolina, a boot camp that graduates an average of 3,400 female Marines per year, according to *Reuters* (Trotta, 2021).

These West Coast recruits in San Diego's Lima Company became the first 53 women to undergo the test, trampling down yet another gender barrier in the U.S. Marine Corps' hesitance to incorporate women into its branch of service. On the historic day, the drill instructors from each platoon granted the female Marines their emblems in a rite of passage. Staff Sergeant Amber Staroscik, the chief drill instructor for Platoon 3241, told the women, "You are part of Marine Corps history" (Trotta, 2021, para. 17).

One of these inspiring women was 20-year-old Abigail Ragland, who'd decided to enlist in the Marine Corps when she heard of its special brotherhood. But now, she said, there would be "a sisterhood."

Abigail Ragland's sisterhood in the U.S. Marine Corps has been years in the making. Hundreds of women came before Ragland and the others in her all-female platoon. The road to becoming a female Marine has been an uphill battle throughout America's history, which required much in exchange. Before these modern-day recruits, women had to make great sacrifices and pave the way for other women, all while dealing with gender inequality, discrimination, and sexism. The trials women faced on their journey were not the trials of male recruits, but these women were victorious despite these tribulations.

This book explores women's history in the Marines and the people and events that led up to women's liberation. To understand how much these women overcame throughout history, it's important to look first at the broad context of historical events, beginning with the first women's rights convention in the mid1800's, through the introduction of female recruits in World War I and World War II. Chapter by chapter, you'll learn more about the characters of our history—their personal stories, their motivations and passions, and the legacy they've left for us all.

To examine the histories of these female pioneers in the Marines, it's crucial to start with a single afternoon tea in New York. Because the women were not automatically allowed in the U.S. Marine Corps, this book is ordered chronologically to easily outline the events that led up to women's service. It also touches on the broader social issues at the time, including fundamental civil rights for women, women's suffrage, and the fight for women's reproductive rights. Woven together in a stunning tapestry are the tales of women's struggle in the Marines and outside of the Marines, as with each decade, a new challenge was wrought, and a new war was fought both literally and figuratively.

The heroines who fought for their place in the Marines Corps are no different than those who fought for women's rights on a broader scale. Each one engaged in a tactical battle for what they believed in, and each one has changed the course of our history and the lives of women in America.

Unfortunately, it's often difficult to find a history book that delivers both facts and an entertaining experience. As you're delving into women's history in the Marines, you may come across a few books that don't expand on the ongoing battle for women's rights. This book offers an extensive view in a concise format and timeline to transport you back in time into these women's stories from the mid-1800's to 2021.

As you journey into the past, you'll learn more about women's rights in Marine Corps history and how the walls against women came down, slowly but surely. By educating yourself on the history of women's rights in and out of the Marines, you'll come away with a greater appreciation for where America is today and perhaps even feel inspired to tackle the issues women still face in the modern world.

From Elizabeth Cady Staton's first call for action upon rights for women to the first women to enlist in the Marines and the formation of the Marine Corps Women's Reserve, you will not only learn about the obstacles each woman faced, but also the reasons behind the struggle, the reluctance of men to accept women as equals, and the work that is still to be done. These women's stories are an inspiration—a beacon that may guide you as you continue on your journey, whether you're simply learning about the Marines, are a current recruit or plan to join.

I have spent years researching women in Marine history and the struggle for women's equality. As a gender historian, I am passionate about bringing these women's stories to life by sparking the reader's imagination and endowing them with the gift of knowledge. Whatever path life takes you, these women's stories—and researching women's history in general—will serve as a reminder to be grateful for where American women are today, as well as an inspiration not to take the status quo.

Even as far as society has come, women are still dealing with inequality in several areas, including the gender wage gap and representation in several career tracks, such as the Marine Corps. The Marine Corps was the last all-male fortification of the U.S. military services. It was only recently the Corps finally accepted that which they couldn't deny any longer—women can enlist, train, and combat equally as men. Today, women comprise about 8% of the officers in the Marines—a number that is still too low compared to other branches. Still, when you think about what it took to get here, you'll find that this number is just a promise of what's to come with the next generations of strong, determined, and ambitious women.

1
CAN A CUP OF TEA CHANGE THE COURSE OF HISTORY?

For much of history, the U.S. Marine Corps was a man's branch of service only, as were the other branches of the U.S. Armed Forces. So it's easy to wonder how women made their place in the Marines, and when the first women thought, "I can do this job just as well as a man can." But, like most questions of women's liberation, you'll need to go a little farther back in history to dive into the roots of its origins.

The date was July 13, 1848. In the high-heat of the summer, a young housewife and mother in upstate New York named Elizabeth Cady Stanton accepted an invitation to tea with four of her female friends. Naturally, the conversation amongst them turned to the situation of women, as it probably still does today. While modern-day women are asking, "When will we receive equal wages to men," Stanton was lamenting about the effects on the social place of women in America following the American Revolution. When the conversation took this turn, Stanton asked her friends, "Hadn't the American Revolution had been fought just 70 years earlier to win the patriots' freedom from tyranny?" (Eisenberg & Ruthsdotter, 1998, para.5). Although these women had taken risks to move across the pond to this new republic, they had not yet received an ounce of extra freedom after enduring the dangerous years of the Revolutionary War.

Not surprisingly, Stanton's friends agreed that American society would greatly benefit from giving women more active roles, but what was a heated conversation over tea and sandwiches was to become a small band of women with a like-minded goal—a goal to incite change.

Just two days following the afternoon tea, Stanton and her friends planned and organized a gathering, readying all the details, including a meeting place and a small advertisement in the Seneca County Courier. They named their convention "A convention to discuss the social, civil, and religious condition and rights of women." It would take place at the Wesleyan Chapel in Seneca Falls, New York, on July 19 and 20, 1848.

Despite the countless conversations between women about their restrictive roles in society, Stanton's tea and subsequent convention marked the first public discussion of women's rights in the history of western civilization.

THE EMERGENCE of the "Declaration of Sentiments"

Stanton went to work drafting what she called the "Declaration of Sentiments." In a moment of patriotism and genius, Stanton used the Declaration of Independence as a model for their document, using its exact lines to bring home the point. "The history of mankind is a history of repeated injuries and usurpations on the part of man toward woman, having in direct object the establishment of an absolute tyranny over her. To prove this, let facts be submitted to a candid world," the document said, just as the Declaration of Independence was in 1776 (National Park Service, 2015, para.3).

From there, Stanton's "Declaration of Sentiments" listed what the women of her age endured.

The modern woman might find it hard to believe how extensive the lack of women's rights was in 1848, but Stanton's list of complaints was lengthy. She drew attention to several points, including the lack of rights once a woman was married (they all reverted to her husband, who essentially owned her as property as far as the laws were concerned), they were not allowed to hold property rights or vote, and they were forced to submit to laws that were enacted without their rightful input.

In Stanton's time, women could scarcely work, and the women who did work had few career options and earned a fraction of the pay a man would receive. Women could not work in higher professions such as medicine or law. The options open to them in 1846 were depressingly domestic, such as becoming a maid, a nanny, a governess (if they received a decent, basic education in primary school), or a cook. Despite the wage inequality, women still had to pay property taxes despite their obvious lack of representation in levying these taxes. As you may have guessed, women could not receive a higher education because colleges and universities would not admit them.

As America was still a man's domain, husbands held legal power over their wives, and at any point they wished they could legally imprison them, beat them, or have them committed to an asylum under the guise of hysteria or madness. If a woman was to divorce her husband, she had no claim to her children because the custody laws favored the man.

The men also had control of their spiritual lives as the women were not allowed to participate in affairs of the church.

In sum, women were at the mercy of men, wholly dependent on them. In Stanton's view, this dependency and lack of civil rights robbed women of their self-confidence and self-respect.

Despite the grave realities these women faced, Stanton was hopeful for change.

The First Women's Rights Convention

On July 19, 1848, Elizabeth Cady Stanton entered Wesleyan Chapel in Seneca Falls. At nine-thirty a.m., she was preparing for the influx of ladies who would show up to discuss what she so hoped to address—women's position in U.S. society. In her advertisement, she asked that only women attend the first day of the event, as she and her friends had planned. Soon, they began to stroll in, some of them looking intrigued, perhaps even incendiary, as they sat there stewing in their thoughts of injustices against them. Some of the ladies, she marked, seemed quite nervous.

As the room filled and the commencement was near, Stanton looked to her friends for support. They nodded, smiled, and in a few seconds, prompted her to take the floor. As she walked to her place, she thought, *I'm just as nervous as a cat.*

She spoke, addressing the crowd, her voice firm and confident:

We are assembled to protest against a form of government, existing without the consent of the governed – to declare our right to be free as man is free, to be represented in the government which we are taxed to support, to have such disgraceful laws as give man the power to chastise and imprison his wife, to take the wages which she earns, the property which she inherits, and, in case of separation, the children of her love; laws test against such unjust laws as these that we are assembled today, and to have them, if possible, forever erased from our statute-books, deeming them as a shame and a disgrace to a Christian republic in the nineteenth century. (Library of Congress, 2015. para. 3)

The first day went off a resounding success in Stanton's mind, although some of the women seemed reluctant. On the second day, July 19, 1848, Stanton again entered the chapel, more inspired even than the day before to reiterate her ideas, reread her declaration, and get people's support. The men walked in with the women, and Stanton felt there must be a change in the air.

On those two summer days in 1848, more than 300 people attended America's first Women's Rights Convention. The two days of discussion yielded 100 signatures on the document, including 32 signatures from men (United States Census Bureau, para. 1). Of the resolutions, 12 received a unanimous endorsement, but the women's right to vote was the sticking point. Women were uncertain of this, and the right to vote in an election was a foreign, radical idea. Even one of Stanton's close friends, Lucretia Mott, thought it shocking to ask for a woman's vote.

The resolution regarding women's voting rights caused so much debate that Stanton could not silence the crowd's arguments. Instead, it took Frederick Douglass, the famous black abolitionist who escaped enslavement in Maryland, to get the crowd's noise to subside.

Such a state of arguing Frederick Douglass had seldom heard. Of course, he'd listened to many heated discussions in his life— and hateful ones at that. But he was too tired to put up with it anymore, and these were civilized people. Men and women who wanted to better the world, mostly. How could they argue that, like the slave, women deserved their freedom?

Finally, he couldn't take it any longer and pulled up his pant legs before climbing up to stand on his chair. He faced the onlookers as they argued and hollered. He wanted them to understand that this issue mattered, and sex and color should not prevent or keep anyone from their freedoms. "Suffrage is the power to choose rulers and make laws and the right by which all others are secured," said Douglass, addressing the crowd. They looked at him, gawking as though a deity had silenced them. There was some more mumbling, but he got them to settle down (Eisenberg & Ruthsdotter, 1998, para. 17).

His convincing testimony helped the resolution by a narrow margin.

Stanton ended her Declaration of Sentiments with a hopeful and realistic statement—they may not see immediate change. Still, this group of women's rights advocates envisioned more conventions, more support, and a rally of women who wanted more.

But, as you may imagine, the first Women's Rights Convention in America didn't go off without a healthy dose of ridicule. Following the two-day event, newspapers, sermons, and editorials beat down the idea with bouts of sarcasm and disbelief. Headlines splashed across the pages included digs like 'The Reign of the Petticoats" and "Insurrection Among the Women." Meanwhile, *The Worcester Telegram* and others perpetuated ideas that these women were radical and even referred to them as "Amazons" who were "bolting with a vengeance." Even more insulting were the mocking reprints of the Declaration of Sentiments and the signatures, including attendees' real names. The press caused such an uproar that many of the convention's attendees were embarrassed.

Imagine being a woman in mid-1800's America, and suddenly after attending this convention for women's rights, your name is splattered in newspapers (by male writers), men laughing at the story, circulating it, mocking it, and using it as common workplace fodder. Meanwhile, your husband (and perhaps the men of your family) are asking you what you were thinking; how could you attend a convention that spewed such radical ideas? Indeed, these responses were a shocking development and not what most of the group expected, and as an essentially helpless woman, you may have been having some second thoughts. Although most of the women stood strong in their position, some of them withdrew their signatures.

Years later, in 1898, Stanton would publish a book titled *Eighty Years and More: Reminiscences 1815-1897*. In it, Stanton described the severity of the backlash, remarking that she and her fellow women were taken aback by the responses. "No words could express what seemed to us so timely, so rational, and so sacred, should be a subject for sarcasm and ridicule to the entire press of the nation," she wrote (Stanton, 1898, pp. 143-144).

However, the saying "There's no such thing as bad press" was true for Stanton and her fight for women's rights. Since the taunting papers had spread the news of what they thought was a ridiculous woman's fancy throughout the country, it brought awareness to people everywhere. Did they support these radical ideas? And if they did, were they, too, up for the fight?

The discussions for women's rights would continue. Though the arguments would not cool down between supporting and nonsupporting sides, Stanton and her comrades had achieved something great: a conversation was ignited across the country and this would lead to progress.

The Continuation of the Women's Rights Movement

After that fateful, two-day event in July 1848, Stanton and the other women of Seneca Falls had hoped to ignite a conversation. They did. Following the first convention, there were several more women's rights conventions held regularly. In fact, for over a decade, between 1850 and the start of the American Civil War in 1861, women's rights conventions convened across the country.

The Seneca Falls Convention ignited a movement for women's rights, and the meetings held throughout the late 19th century addressed those issues Stanton put into writing.

Other women who would emerge as leaders of the movement included Susan B. Anthony, Matilda Joslyn Gage, Lucy Stone, and the black abolitionist and women's rights advocate Sojourner Truth. These women would dedicate much of their lives to campaigning for the future generations of women, some 40 years of organizing events and spreading the hope that women's civil rights would become a reality.

One of these pioneers was a strong ally for Stanton. They met before the Civil War in 1850, when Susan B. Anthony was a teacher in Massachusetts. After the civil war, both Stanton and Anthony would help form a movement for women's suffrage, turning the idea of the women's vote into one of the main issues of the Women's Rights Movement. By now, the women advocating for their civil rights knew that the power to vote would enable them to achieve other victories. So when the Reconstruction era came, these two women would push lawmakers to include women's rights.

Unfortunately, when they wrote the Fourteenth Amendment, it would again leave out women, despite the work that Stanton and her comrades had done. But Stanton didn't take it without a fight.

Stanton and Anthony took action concerning the Fourteenth Amendment before it became a constitutional law.

On a cold winter day on January 23, 1866, Representative James Brooks of New York received a petition from Stanton and a letter crafted by Anthony. He and the rest of Congress argued over the document—some of the men likely remarked, "Government and law are no place for women. That's a man's domain." But others were receptive, including a George Washington Julian of Indiana, who decided he would take action for these women. In December 1868, Julian took the floor of Congress, two winters later, and proposed a constitutional amendment that would be more inclusive. Julian asked that the right to vote would be "without any distinction or discrimination whatever founded on race, color, or sex" (U.S. House of Representatives, 2007, para. 5). In an atmosphere full of powerful men in government, you can almost hear the tension that must have followed. By extending the right to vote to women, their government and social boundaries would begin to alter, and this wasn't favorable for most 19th century men. Most of Congress hated the idea so much that Julian's resolution never made it to the voting process and was disdainfully tossed aside.

Rome was not built in a day, and neither was the arduous path for women's suffrage. It would take 72 years for success, and when it did finally happen, it was due to the sweat and tears of women and male supporters' work in organizing, taking action, and lobbying.

The movement included many followers of what Stanton and her afternoon tea had started. The pioneers who followed included Esther Morris, who led the first successful state campaign for women's suffrage in Wyoming in 1869. She would become the first woman to hold a judicial position on February 14, 1870.

One Abigail Scott Duniway successfully fought for women's voting rights in Oregon and Washington in the early 1900's. Fighting for suffrage for all women were the African American women Ida B. Wells-Barnett (also one a founder of the National Association for the Advancement of Colored People) and Mary Church Terrell, one of the first-ever African American women to earn a college degree.

Both Lucy Stone's daughter and Elizabeth Cady Stanton's daughter followed in their mothers' footsteps and advocated for women's suffrage in the late 1800's and early 1900's.

Women also have to thank Anna Howard Shaw and Carrie Chapman Catt. They led the National American Woman Suffrage Association in the early 20th century and helped usher in success for the movement. The founder of the National Woman's Party, Alice Paul, also helped bring the women's vote to reality.

Finally, in September 1918, President Woodrow Wilson came before the Senate and asked for women's right to vote. His address was two months before the end of World War I. Many women had successfully joined the war effort, working as stenographers, messengers, truck drivers, mechanics, cryptographers, clerks, radio operators, and more. Over 11,000 women joined the United States Navy to serve their country from March 1917 to the end of the war in November 1918 (National Park Service, 2018). Before then, women began serving war efforts through service organizations as early as August 1914.

There was Wilson, the 28th President of the United States, taking the Senate floor. The once awkward public speaker—who had blossomed into a great orator years earlier—eloquently addressed his comrades in government. With passion, Woodrow asked, "We have made partners of the women in this war; shall we admit them only to a partnership of suffering and sacrifice and toil and not to a partnership of privilege and right?" (Lange, 2016, para. 2). Finally, Congress passed the 19th Amendment in June 1919, which gave citizens, no matter what sex, the right to vote. The amendment was ratified on August 18, 1920.

The right to vote, of course, didn't automatically allow women to join male-led careers such as the U.S. Marine Corps. Although women would serve in war efforts for WWI and WWII, many government officials saw it as temporary.

Years later, the country would change under such influences as Ruth Bader Ginsburg, the late Supreme Court Justice, who worked tirelessly to increase women's rights during her career. There are many ways to sum up the vital history of women suffragettes, but Ginsburg's tribute perhaps said it best. "I think about how much we owe to the women who went before us—legions of women, some known but many more unknown. I applaud the bravery and resilience of those who helped all of us—you and me—to be here today" (Eisenberg & Ruthsdotter, 1998, para. 25).

To pay homage to these female pioneers, you must place yourself in 1914, as women were still fighting for women's suffrage at the start of WWI where a woman named Opha May Johnson would become the first woman to join the Marines.

TIMELINE OF EVENTS **Leading Up To Women Marine's History:**

- Elizabeth Cady Stanton discusses the lack of civil rights women have during a friendly afternoon tea on July 14, 1848.
- The first Women's Rights Convention took place in Seneca Falls, New York, on July 19 and 20, 1848.
- Two years after the first Women's Rights Convention in
- Seneca Falls, the first National Women's Rights Convention was held at Brinley Hall in Worcester, Massachusetts, on October 23 and 24 in 1850. The second National Women's Rights Convention began on October 15 and 16, 1851, presided by Paulina Kellogg Wright Davis. The convention includes a reading of a letter from Elizabeth Cady Stanton. The third

National Woman's Rights Convention occurred over three days—September 8, 9, and 10,—in 1852 at City Hall in Syracuse, New York. Lucretia Mott presides over the convention, which was called to further the movement's plan to secure women's social and civil rights.

- Seven more National Women's Rights Conventions occurred in subsequent years leading up to 1863. The first Woman's National Loyal League Convention took place on May 14, 1863, in New York City, where Susan B. Anthony tells the attendees, "It is not because women suffer, it is not because slaves suffer ... it is the simple assertion of the great fundamental truth of democracy that was proclaimed by our Revolutionary fathers" (More Women's Rights Conventions, 2015, para. 37).
- The U.S Civil War began on April 12, 1861.
- On April 9, 1865, the Civil War ended.
- Opha May Johnson was born on May 4, 1878. Opha May Johnson is the first woman to enlist in the U.S. Marine Corps on August 13, 1918.

2

OPHA MAY JOHNSON: THE FIRST FEMALE MARINE

On June 28, 1914, cries broke out across Austria. "The Archduke is dead! He was assassinated!" Archduke Franz Ferdinand of Austria and his wife Sophie had traveled to Bosnia to the capital city of Sarajevo. There, they planned to inspect the imperial troops stationed there. However, Austria-Hungary had annexed Bosnia in 1908, and Serbians were not happy about it (McDermott, 2018, paras.1-4).

On the way to the city, the Archduke and his wife escaped a bomb from Serbian terrorists. Later in the day, a 19-year-old Serbian nationalist, Gavrilo Princip, shot and killed the Archduke and his wife. Ferdinand's assassination angered Austria-Hungary, and a month later, on July 28, 1914, alongside allied countries Germany, Bulgaria, and the Ottoman Empire, they declared war on Serbia.

In this first World War, the United States would ally alongside Great Britain, France, Russia, Italy, Romania, and Japan. During this time of multinational bloodshed, women still could not vote and felt powerless against the threat of war. The only thing for a woman to do was to lie down and take it or help. Although women suffragettes had not yet earned the say-so in their country's government, they were patriotic at heart. They wanted the United States of America to be an inclusive, fair country—one where women could help during a call-to-arms. These women, who still did not have many fundamental civil rights, wanted nothing more than to be seen as equal to men, and thus, serving their country was what they did.

During WWI, nearly 25,000 women from 21 to 69 would serve overseas, while a whopping 35,000 assisted with war efforts in total (U.S. Army, 2016).

So, in August 1914, women began going into service, starting with a few single women. Soon, service organizations would recruit women to help. But the U.S. government would not request help from women to officially serve in a military capacity until 1917. These women often served as nurses, but they also filled other jobs, such as administrative and secretarial positions.

The war would officially end in 1918—and cries of triumph broke out when the allied powers won. Women joined the celebrations, but the catastrophic amount of bloodshed in the wake of the war was a difficult reality.

Despite serving their country, in 1918, American women had still not earned the right to vote. Nonetheless, many women continued to serve in the armed forces following Armistice Day; some did not return home until 1923.

As their heroic efforts off the battlefield were history-making in America, their contributions didn't go unnoticed. Because of these efforts, President Woodrow Wilson confronted the Senate, reminding his colleagues in government that the women served throughout the war, and they deserved a say in their country's operations.

Thanks to the inspiring women of WWI, the 19th Amendment passed on June 4, 1919, but its ratification would not happen until 1920.

Women served the war in several capacities, but some of the most interesting occurred when the U.S. government officially recruited them. In France, the United States Army recruited bilingual women to operate the telephones and work switchboards. These women, who became the first female American soldiers, earned the nickname "The Hello Girls." Once trained, these women were off to Europe in March 1918 alongside their Chief Operator Grace Banker. Although these female telephone operators put their lives on the line in France, like the men of the Army, they didn't receive the title of a U.S. Army member. The women didn't receive army benefits that male soldiers did, and they also had to pay for their uniforms.

Most of this information was unbeknownst to these women, who all believed they had officially enlisted in the army. After Armistice Day, the Hello Girls found out that they weren't technically a part of the military but civilian contractors due to Army regulations that required soldiers to be male. Years later, in 1979, Congress recognized the Hello Girls as WWI veterans by law. However, it took nearly 100 years for "The Hello Girls" to be inducted into the U.S. Army Women's Hall of Fame in 2019.

Due to the shortages of men in the Navy, the United States Secretary of the Navy, Josephus Daniels, used a loophole in the Naval Act of 1916 to allow women to enlist. Because it did not specify that only men could enlist, in March 1917, he began enlisting women. They were called yeoman, and the length of lines at recruiting stations may have surprised you. Hundreds of young women from 18 to 35 went to enlist, and when the U.S. officially entered WWI combat on April 6, 1917, there were two thousand women enlisted in the Navy. By the time the war ended, the Navy's total number of female yeomen had hit 11,000 (Toler, 2019, para.4).

Although they were supposed to do clerical duties only, as the war continued, female yeoman would also serve as supervisors for naval shipments, fingerprint experts, pharmacists, torpedo assemblers, and even camouflage designers. These yeomen were also trained to march and perform basic military drills to help raise money at war bond drives and morale at troops send-offs.

The women, registered officially as "Yeomen (F)," received the nickname "Yeomanettes" from the American media, which Daniels disliked. Compared to women enlisted in the U.S. Army, the women in the Navy received better pay, benefits, and insurance—the same as their male counterparts.

In 1918, the U.S. Marine Corps opened its branch of service to women. Their advertisements asked for "women of excellent character and neat appearance, with business and office experience" (Kratz, 2017, para.4).

The patriotic feeling in the air was so thick, you could have cut it with a knife, and 40-year-old Opha May Jacob Johnson took it all in. But before discussing Johnson's decision to join the Marine Corps, it's essential to talk about her life leading up to 1918.

Opha May Johnson was born in Kokomo, Indiana, on May 4, 1878—thirty years after Elizabeth Cady Stanton's organized women's rights convention. Johnson was raised in Washington, D.C., attended Wood's Commercial College, and graduated second in her class (out of 37 students) in 1895. An article in *The Washington Times* reported, "the salutatorian, Miss Opha Jacob, entertained the audience with a carefully prepared paper" at the graduation ceremony (The Washington Times, 1895, p.4).

Johnson had never been so proud as to address the crowd at her graduation. They cheered, and she felt such a future on the horizon as if she could reach out and taste it. There were so many possibilities, and although she wasn't quite sure what she was to do yet, she knew that she wanted to do something big, something that would make a change in the world.

As she bid her fellow graduates farewell, she felt incandescent —a feeling that she hoped would help her illuminate the path before her.

Four years later, Johnson was getting ready to be married. Victor Hugo Johnson was a firecracker—one she thought would help her on her way to greatness. Victor was a music director for the Lafayette Square Opera House in Washington, D.C., and the romance that came along with a musician was unparalleled. He merely had to break down music theory for her, and she was sunk like a pirate ship.

Just five days before Christmas, in 1898, Opha felt she would burst as she looked into the mirror at her reflection. There she was, all clad in white, about to walk the union of her life. And she was ready for it.

Johnson was a bright-minded, determined woman with an open and friendly face. Her eyes sparkled with intelligence, and a glance at her photo leaves the impression that she would have set out to do many great things—if a lifetime of other possibilities had been open to her. This determined spirit is perhaps what led her down the path of making history in the Marine Corps. After her marriage to Victor, Opha began working in civil service in the Interstate Commerce Department, serving as a clerk to the Quartermaster General in the United States Army. In her position, she assisted the Quartermaster General (likely George H.

Weeks or Marshall I. Ludington) with his documentation, as the U.S. Army's Quartermaster is in charge of the quartermaster units and personnel and their supplies, doctrine, and training. Her position there would continue for 14 years.

How Johnson reached her decision to join the U.S. Marine Corps is unclear, but one leading theory is someone invited her to become a recruit.

Joining The Marines

Nancy Wilt of the Women Marines Association searched for answers in 2005. Her theory lays out Johnson's story something like this: Johnson received an invitation to join the U.S. Marines and decided to take it. She went to take her physical exam on August 12 and passed and officially signed her enlistment papers on the following day, August 13, 1918.

Unfortunately, Wilt and her colleagues uncovered little other supporting documents that show why Johnson decided to join the Marines. "I felt there was very little history of women Marines preserved," Wilt told *Time Magazine* (Waxman, 2018, para.5). Research about Johnson's life and enlistment yielded no diaries or personal records that revealed Johnson's feelings or motivations.

Wilt, however, thinks Johnson was invited because of her outstanding administrative skills and her top marks. Whatever the case, Johnson enlisted and signed her paper. In her contract, they had to scratch out the male pronouns throughout and change them to female—the first time someone needed to alter the male pronouns to accommodate a woman.

Johnson walked out of the recruitment office, the first woman to join the Marines. It was a surreal feeling, no doubt, but she would not be the only female Marine to join during WWI. Johnson was one of 300 women recruited for office jobs at the Marine Corps headquarters. In the throes of WWI, they needed more men in France, working on the frontlines. To make this possible, they brought in the "Marinettes," the nickname for this first group of female U.S. Marines. Some of these women also supported nurses fighting the battle of a pandemic—the 1918 influenza outbreak.

Marinettes held the nickname until WWII, when these working women finally earned the respect of male officers. One of the Marines to explicitly honor the women Marines was Major General Commandant Thomas Holcomb. He told LIFE magazine in 1944: "They don't have a nickname, and they don't need one. They get their basic training in a Marine atmosphere at a Marine post. They inherit the traditions of Marines. They are Marines" (Time INC., 1944, p. 81).

Johnson excelled in her position and received a promotion to Sergeant on September 18, 1918. Unfortunately, there's little else known about her throughout the rest of her career. She remained on active duty until February 1919—presumably taking an even better clerical position.

Although she never shipped out of D.C.'s Marine headquarters, her contributions to women in the Marine Corps were (and still are) undeniable. In 1943, Johnson officially retired from government service at the age of 65. Twelve years later, on August 11, 1955, Johnson died. She was buried in an unmarked grave, having no children, no nephews or nieces, and no young relatives.

Despite her lifetime achievements, Johnson was essentially forgotten — even by the females following her footsteps as Marines. The reason is probably a compound one—the lack of documentation for these first female Marines, no recovered personal records, and the end of her life being an unassuming, rather sad conclusion in a grave with no headstone.

THE IMPORTANCE of Johnson's Legacy

One retired major, Kathy Shepard, who served for 20 years as a communication officer in the Marines, says she had no idea who Johnson was. "I didn't find out about her until several years after I had been in the Marine Corps. No one had taken the time to research it until Nancy [Wilt] did" (Waxman, 2018, para.11).

Deep into her research, Wilt received information about where Opha May Johnson's grave might be. When she did find the location, she and her colleagues spent a year raising money to erect an obelisk monument marking her grave in Rock Creek Cemetery in Washington, D.C., and it finally became a reality on August 29, 2018. The memorial's unveiling was a ceremony fit for the first female Marine, complete with a Marine brass quintet.

It's an essential piece of American history, and Johnson excelled at what she did. Although she has a monument, and it's possible more people know her name, it's a story that needs to be told and retold, as these female pioneers deserve the credit for getting American women as far as they have come.

The Continuation of Women's Rights and Women's Role in the Marines 1913-1918:

- Alice Paul and Lucy Burns founded the Congressional Union for Woman Suffrage (CU) in April 1913.
- World War I began on July 28, 1914.
- Women join civil service through various organizations beginning in 1914 after the war starts.
- Women began enlisting in the Navy as yeomen in March 1917.
- The United States entered the war as an official ally in battle on April 6, 1917.
- The "Spanish flu" pandemic began in 1918.
- In March 1918, female U.S. Army recruits ship off to
- Europe after training as "Hello Girls."
- In 1918, the Marine Corps opened its branch of service to women, and on August 13, Opha May Johnson officially enlisted as the first woman Marine. A total of 300 women enlist in the U.S. Marines after Johnson does in late summer and fall 1918. On September 18, 1918, the Navy promoted Johnson to Sergeant.
- In 1919, the National American Woman Suffrage Association changed its name to the League of Women Voters in anticipation of the suffrage victory. Women won the right to vote with the 19th Amendment on June 4, 1919.
- The 19th Amendment was ratified into law on August 18, 1920.

3
THE TRUE FIGHT FOR WOMEN'S RIGHTS BEGINS

Although Elizabeth Cady Stanton did not live to see women win the right to vote (she died on October 26, 1902), the events that led up to the 19th Amendment's ratification would have made her proud. Finally, after the years of toil, women had earned the right to vote, thanks to President Woodrow Wilson's recognition of women's war efforts in WWI.

However, the real work was not Wilson's, but the women who came before, such as Stanton and her group of friends who refused to lie down and give up their human rights.

After the House of Representatives passed the 19th Amendment on May 21, 1919, following Woodrow's call-to-action, the Senate would pass it two weeks later. It took time for the 19th Amendment to become official, but once Tennessee became the 36th state to ratify it on August 18, 1920, the battle was won. This brought the tally of ratifications to three-quarters, and thus, Secretary of State Bainbridge Colby certified the ratification days later, on August 26, 1920.

The day the amendment passed was a joyous day for women across the United States (and perhaps even fearful for those who were still reluctant). Imagine the joy of overcoming a years-long fight, which began long before your activism, one that American women knew their grandmothers would revel in. You can almost hear them shouting for joy through the streets, dancing on cobblestones, anticipating the first time they could attend an election and fill out a ballot. But, unfortunately, this elation would not last because as the celebrations fizzled, women were left with the question, "What now?"

Yes, they had the right to vote. But soon, women realized that although they won this battle, there were more to come. While voting is a quintessential backbone to freedom, these women were still not equal to men.

Once women won the vote, the Women's Rights Movement still had work to do. Unfortunately, many supporters of women's suffrage thought the vote was enough and didn't continue their fight for civil rights. However, several people did realize the significance of going further.

The National American Woman Suffrage Association, now the League of Women Voters since 1919, hoped to inspire women to make their vote count now that it was official. Other changes were also brewing. The Women's Bureau of the Department of Labor was established in 1920 to analyze women's roles and treatment in the workforce while also championing legislation that would make these changes, ensuring women had a safe and fair work environment.

Three years after women's right to vote was officially established, Alice Paul, who led the National Woman's Party, drafted an Equal Rights Amendment for the U.S. Constitution in 1923. Paul called the amendment the "Lucretia Mott Amendment" to honor Mott's work in women's rights. The purpose of this amendment was to bring total equality between men and women. It read: "Men and women shall have equal rights throughout the United States and every place subject to its jurisdiction" (Equal Rights Amendment–Alice Paul Institute, n.d., para. 1). Since the law would be at a federal level, every state would have to recognize equality. However, Paul's Amendment was too progressive at the time and would have an arduous history in Congress.

Before getting into the outcome of her Equal Rights Amendment, however, it's important to understand what made Alice tick and why she wanted absolute equality to come to fruition.

. . .

The Silent Sentinels

Alice Paul was the firstborn daughter of a Quaker businessman William Paul and his wife Tacie Perry, born on January 11, 1885. Her absolute determination to bring gender equality to a federal level is traceable to her childhood.

Her father was wealthy, and although he was a devout Quaker, the New Jersey resident and his wife were avid believers of gender rights and equality.

One can only imagine Alice, the eldest of four, growing up alongside her siblings and sitting around the fire, hearing her father talk of ideas such as women's education and how a good hard day's work improves society. Although these were unusual stances in their time, particularly for a man, Paul's family must have made it seem like a common ideal.

Strengthening little Alice's grit, her mother Tacie was a devout suffragist and even brought Alice along to her women's suffrage meetings.

When she grew older, Alice Paul attended Swarthmore College, graduated with a degree in biology in 1905, and received a Master of Arts degree in society from the New York School of Philanthropy in 1907. If that wasn't enough, this incredible woman studied social work in England and received a Ph.D. from the University of Pennsylvania in 1912, after returning to America in 1910. Although it seems almost unheard of for women of the early 1900's to earn a Ph.D., Paul was not the first to do so. The first woman to graduate with a Ph.D. in the United States was Helen Magill White in 1877, who studied Greek and wrote a dissertation titled The Greek Drama.

During her stay in England, Paul met Lucy Burns—a fellow suffragette—and got into the women's suffrage efforts there. How they met, however, was a real show of their characters.

There was a great, bustling crowd outside of the United Kingdom's Parliament building. The scene may have reminded Alice of her mother's suffrage meetings, where she attended as a girl, listening contentedly to the words that seemed to define her from that first time. Now, she was in London, and she'd heard there was a protest for women's suffrage.

Gladly, she decided to attend. The air, thick with tension, was full of women's chants and yells, arms pumping upward. The sight was passionate but peaceful.

As the crowd got rowdier, soon there was the sound of whistles, cutting into the atmosphere. Alice hardly knew what was happening until she was arrested.

Inside the police station, Paul and her fellow protesters were shoved into a holding cell, and she met a woman who hardly looked phased by the day's events. This woman was Lucy Burns, who had already been arrested four times prior during her work with Emmeline and Christabel Pankhurst's Women's Social and Political Union (WSPU), which was the leading militant organizing campaign for women's suffrage in the United Kingdom. The WSPU's tactics included smashing windows, committing arson, and sometimes taunting politicians.

Alice began talking to Lucy and immediately knew she'd found a friend and ally in this fearless creature.

Paul and Burns would go on to work together with the National American Woman Suffrage Association (NAWSA) on its Congressional Committee once back in the United States. Because the pair worked together so well, they would found the Congressional Union for Woman Suffrage (CU) in April 1913, later known as the National Woman's Party (NWP).

The battle up to the moment Paul wrote the Equal Rights Amendment was a long road, full of further protests, organizing, confronting, and imprisonment.

In October 1917, after peacefully picketing in front of the White House during President Woodrow Wilson's term, Alice found herself sentenced to seven months in prison. The lead-up to that event was a slew of other protests and an increasingly bitter taste in Woodrow's mouth. Despite his lukewarm support of women's voting rights, he was annoyed at the NWP's persistence, especially during wartime, where other groups ceased protests to focus on wartime efforts.

These women of the NWP earned the name the "Silent Sentinels" and were often outside the White House gates for six days in a row before Paul's incarceration. One sign specifically called out Wilson, reading, "Mr. President, how long must women wait for liberty?" (Wagner, n.d, para.3). On October 20, 1917, Alice Paul was arrested after waving her banner, which featured a direct quote from President Wilson.

Although there had been several arrests before Alice's prison stint, the stakes began to rise higher and higher each time, and the constant protests made President Wilson become increasingly impatient, even though the demonstrations were peaceful ones. There was also dissatisfaction from other Americans, who saw the coverage of these protests in the press and thought the Silent Sentinels to be unpatriotic and disrespectful to continue fighting for women's suffrage during a time of war. Alice's non-violent, Quaker upbringing had led her to prefer non-militant tactics, such as peaceful protesting. Yet, this is what resulted in her prison experience and the other terrors her friends would face in a minimum-security facility.

Several days after the arrest of these 33 women, authorities transferred some to the District Jail, like Paul, and many others to the Occoquan Workhouse in Lorton, Virginia.

Alice Paul arrived at the District Jail that October and soon found herself in solitary confinement for two weeks. She waited there in the dark at night, her stomach growling in hunger. They only gave her bread and water, and she could feel the weight slipping off of her with each day that passed. Soon, it became easy to go without food. The pangs of her stomach hurt as she hurt for the freedoms of women, which weren't realized, no matter their protests.

When the end of her two weeks came, Alice was so weak that she could barely lift her head off her pillow. The warden then moved her to the prison hospital, alarmed at the gauntness of her cheeks. But she had already gone so long without the necessary nutrition, so she began to talk to the other women in the hospital, organizing a hunger strike.

Of course, the doctors saw that they weren't eating. Soon, Alice had to fight them off her as they forced a tube down her throat. She and the other women were nearly made sick with the mixture. They told her she was close to being committed to an asylum. *So be it*, she thought.

When Paul and her comrades in the District Jail executed their hunger strike, the doctors' high-protein diet fed to them through tubes was often too much for their stomachs, causing them further distress through vomiting.

Meanwhile, the Silent Sentinels at the Occoquan experienced their own horrors. The minimum-security prison focused more on reform, work, and productivity than isolation and physical punishment. However, the setting was not a haven for these women and didn't guarantee a safer, more humane place, despite its advertisement. On November 14, an event occurred that earned the nickname "The Night of Terror." Many of the women involved would shock the press with their recitations of the tale.

When many of the Silent Sentinels, including Lucy Burns, were sent to the Occoquan Workhouse, they would demand to be treated as political prisoners, which didn't go over well with the prison's superintendent William H. Whittaker. So Whittaker decided the Sentinels needed a firm hand and ordered his guards to take care of the situation.

Their stay at Occoquan began with the guards "bursting into the room where the women were waiting to be booked," only to be "dragged down the hall and [thrown] into dark, filthy cells" (Pruitt, 2019, para.17).

What followed is a scene out of a nightmare. The indignities the suffragettes faced included a forced strip and hose-down, scratchy uniforms, and abusive acts. Lucy Burns found herself shackled to the ceiling of her cell, threatened with a straitjacket and a gag. She stood through the night; her hands cuffed tightly so that she couldn't lay down. Silent Sentinel Dorothy Day was picked up by two guards and slammed onto an iron bench.

One of the women, Dorothy Lewis, had her head smashed into an iron bed. When her comrade, Alice Cosu, saw this violent act, she suffered a heart attack. But, cruelly, the guards didn't advocate for her medical attention, and Cosu didn't receive any until the following morning.

The escalation in violence was only some of the cruelty they faced at the workhouse. There, the food was crawling with worms. "The beans, hominy, rice, cornmeal...and cereal have all had worms in them," said Virginia Bovee in Doris Stevens' memoir, Jailed For Freedom (1920, p.145).

Many of the suffragettes at the Occoquan also engaged in hunger strikes. Eventually, the news of the cruelty there reached the public. In late November 1917, authorities released the prisoners from custody, including Alice Paul and Lucy Burns. Only months later, in early 1918, the D.C. Court of Appeals ruled in the women's favor—they had been illegally arrested and imprisoned.

After these events, President Wilson began to change his tune and start advocating for the 19th Amendment.

Unfortunately for Paul, after the 19th Amendment passed and the states ratified it on August 18, 1920, her fight was not over. Her Equal Rights Amendment was introduced for consideration to the U.S. Congress in 1923, but it wasn't presented for a vote. Introduced each year through 1970, the Equal Rights Amendment was only presented for a vote in 1946. That year, the Senate voted against it.

The Fight for Reproductive Rights

While Alice Paul and her Silent Sentinels were sacrificing to make women's suffrage a reality, women in the United States also began to realize they lacked another right—the right to control their bodies.

Although modern women may take access to birth control and contraceptive care for granted, there was a time when women had no access to it whatsoever. It's also important to note that access to birth control is still a hotly debated topic; and although the country has come a long way, some women still don't have the proper access to reproductive care due to different state laws.

Although Elizabeth Cady Stanton and her supporters did excellent work, there was no mention of women's reproductive health in the Declaration of Sentiments. But one day, a public health nurse named Margaret Sanger would become a pivotal figure in the fight for women's reproductive rights.

Around the same time, the suffragettes were close to achieving their goal of the women's right to vote. Sanger desired another women's liberation.

Sanger grew up in Corning, New York, born September 14, 1879. Because she was a middle child of 11 siblings and severely shaped by poverty in her youth, she would pursue a cause for women's rights. A driving force in Sanger's beliefs also came from the death of her mother,

Anna Purcell Higgens, who passed away at 50 after physical issues from her nearly one dozen pregnancies.

In 1896, Sanger pursued nursing at Claverack College and Hudson River Institute. In 1902, she completed the nursing program at White Plains Hospital. When Margaret married architect William Sanger that year, she relocated to Hastings, New York. Margaret mothered three children and believed that mothers who wanted children would raise a better generation than those who had them by accident or even begrudgingly for lack of birth control access.

Once in Hastings, she and her husband joined Progressive Era activists in groups, including the Women's Committee of the New York chapter of the Socialist Party. The Sangers met alongside other intellectuals organizing for progressive reform, such as Upton Sinclair (the future governor of California) and Max Eastman (a poet and political activist).

What spurred Margaret Sanger on was her knowledge of women's poverty and its indisputable link to unexpected pregnancies. During her time, however, promoting the knowledge of birth control methods was illegal. As a nurse, she saw many large families, poor immigrants, and wives who experienced health issues due to pregnancies. Included in these women were those who had undergone illegal abortions or were pregnant too many times than was good for their body.

Soon, Sanger's mission was to help these women by providing them with information about birth control. She also wished to repeal the federal Comstock Law of 1873—a law that made it illegal to distribute "obscene, lewd or lascivious," "immoral," or "indecent" material through the mail (Burnette, 2009, para. 1). The Comstock Law also made giving, selling, or possessing one of these books, advertisements, pamphlets, pictures, or drawings— including anything on contraception or abortion, despite if it was from a medical professional—a misdemeanor offense.

Despite this law, Sanger published a feminist journal called The Woman Rebel in 1914—a decision that resulted in her charge for violating the Comstock Law. She escaped her trial by fleeing to England but would return to the United States to stand trial a year later. However, the judge would drop the charges after the public began advocating for her following the death of her five-year-old daughter.

Although these charges against Sanger disappeared, in 1916, a week after she opened the first birth control clinic in Brownsville, Brooklyn, authorities arrested her. She even distributed a pamphlet, which advertised her clinic. It read, "Mothers! Can you afford to have a large family? Do you want any more children? If not, why do you have them?" The pamphlet concluded by explaining they could prevent pregnancy: "Do not kill, do not take life, but prevent. Safe, harmless information can be obtained of trained nurses at 46 Amboy Street, near Pitkin Ave. — Brooklyn" (Straughn, n.d., para. 1).

Margaret thought of the women who suffered, even died, because they had too many babies. Babies they didn't even want. Sometimes, she thought of her own children and how loved they were. Then, she thought of her beautiful daughter, who'd been taken from her too soon. Finally, she stood inside the birth control clinic feeling a sense of accomplishment at her work.

But then she heard the noises outside, and the police were knocking on her door again.

Her arrest, this time, got her 30 days in jail. There were some well-known supporters of Sanger's work, and her arrest had again prompted the media to break out the typewriters. She tried to appeal but lost. However, her loss wasn't without a victory. During her trial, the courts ruled in favor of women with medical reasons, making physician prescriptions for contraceptives legal when vital to their heath. This would allow Sanger to open another clinic in 1923, where she staffed female social workers and doctors. Her clinic would eventually become the Planned Parenthood Federation of America.

It wouldn't be until 1936 that the courts would make birth control prescriptions for all women legal. And it would take even longer for the Comstock laws to end—they finally did in 1971.

Sanger's revolutionary views led to even more freedoms for women, but they took time. Meanwhile, women fighting for these rights could only take action in the streets, Congress, the media, and protests and words. They were not allowed to fight in real wars, but the opportunity would come.

World War II would loom on the horizon, an impending threat. When the conflict between world powers was apparent, Congresswoman Edith Nourse Rogers of Massachusetts spoke out. When realizing that women would likely serve again (though perhaps not in the same capacity as men), Rogers asserted her determination to make a change. "I was resolved that our women would not again serve with the Army without the same protection the men got," she said (United States Army, 2016, para. 18). Her work led to the formation of the Women's Army Corps.

It would take time, but women were eventually included in WWII in more vital roles instead of only in administration. They still weren't allowed to fight as the men were.

In the Army, women began WWII in various fields, such as cryptography, military intelligence, maintenance and supply, parachute rigging, and nursing. Nurses were perhaps the most common, as over 60,000 Army Nurses served in WII around the world. From the day WWII broke out on September 1, 1939, to its end on September 2, 1945, 140,000 women had enlisted and served in the Women's Army Corps and the U.S. Army (United States Army, 2016).

Rogers also fought to establish a women's auxiliary corps shortly after the bombing of Pearl Harbor. On May 14, 1942, President Franklin D. Roosevelt created and signed the Women's Army Auxiliary Corps (WAAC). Over a year later, on July 1, 1943, the WAAC's name was changed to the Women's Army Corps (WAC).

Women's role in WWII began a revolution, bringing about economic and social changes that transformed their roles in U.S. society. Soon, it would become more common for women to work and serve.

When the Imperial Japanese Navy Air Service attacked the U.S. naval base at Pearl Harbor in Honolulu, Hawaii, on December 7, 1941, change was imminent.

WOMEN IN THE MARINES 1942-1947:

- On October 31, 1942, the Secretary of the Navy, Frank Knox, authorized a Marine Corps Women's Reserve (MCWR) to assist with WWII.

- The Commandant Lieutenant General Thomas Holcomb approves the formation of the MCWR on November 7, 1942.
- In 1943, Colonel Ruth Cheney Street became the first Director of the MCWR.
- The first commissioned officer for the MCWR was Captain Anne Lentz in 1943.
- On February 13, 1943, enlistments for the Women's Reserve officially opened, and Private Lucille McClarren became the first woman to enlist. In March 1943, MCWR officer candidates and MCWR enlistees began training with the Navy's Women Accepted for Volunteer Emergency Service (WAVES) at the U.S. Naval Midshipmen's School in Massachusetts, and the U.S. Naval Training School at Hunter College in New York, respectively.
- On April 25, 1943, the first class of official female
- Marines in the MCWR reported active duty. On May 4, the first class of Officer candidates graduate and report to duty.
- On February 13, 1944, the MCWR had its first anniversary.
- 160 enlisted women Marines and five women officers arrived in Hawaii for duty on January 29, 1945. On September 2, 1945, WWII ended, a few months after V-E Day on May 7.
- The Marine Corps set the MCWR termination date for September 1, 1946, with the idea that women shouldn't remain in the Marines after wartime.
- On March 17, 1947, Sergeant Mary Frances Wancheck was the first woman Marine to rate a "hash mark."

4

THE EMERGENCE OF FEMALES IN THE
MARINES

U.S. Massachusetts Rep. Edith Nourse Rogers was a spitfire. WWII was well underway in 1941. Before the war had begun, she knew that the government would again call on its women to assist in another devastating worldwide war. However, she didn't want them to be taken advantage of again, as they were in the case of the Hello Girls in the U.S. Army.

Because of this, she introduced a bill for the formation of the Women's Army Auxiliary Corps (WAAC). After the tragic attack on Pearl Harbor, the U.S. Congress approved the bill on May 14, 1942, President Franklin D. Roosevelt signed it into law the following day, and the WAAC was a go. Its first director was Oveta Culp Hobby—a journalist, politician, and civil servant from Killeen, Texas—who was officially sworn in on May 16, 1942.

Upon its creation, the WAAC was established to provide women with national defense skills, knowledge, and training. Not unironically, the WAAC chose Greek goddess Pallas Athene as its insignia, the figure who stood for victory, feminine virtue, and the art of war. Members of the WAAC wore Athene's image on their lapels, alongside the traditional U.S. emblem, and an eagle on their caps to represent the Army bird.

Later in the WAAC's history, they would call the eagle "the Buzzard," visible also on their uniforms' buttons.

When the first women of the WAAC arrived at the training center in Fort Des Moines, Iowa, it was a sticky, humid July in 1942. The crowd totaled some 565 women: 125 enlistees and 440 officer applicants. These women, including 40 black women, were selected to attend the new WAAC Officer Candidate School (OCS) and undergo Army training. In total, more than 35,000 U.S. women applied for the WAAC during its first recruiting drive (United States Army, 2016).

You can imagine this new sparked renewed interest in women's civil rights and how this integration could affect the future generations of Americans. Nonetheless, even though the WAAC was a triumph, the women weren't governed directly by the Articles of War or Army regulations. Moreover, although WAAC enlistees earned the income, these women still didn't receive overseas pay or government-paid life insurance, which meant no gratuities. Should they die, the burden of funeral costs was still on their relatives.

Rogers would soon take further action. In January 1943, Rep. Rogers introduced a bill to both houses of Congress. This time, the bill asked for women's right to enlist in the U.S. Army or Reserves. Upon acceptance, this bill would mean women would be allowed to serve overseas, granting them equal rank, benefits, and privileges as Army men.

Although its first recruiting efforts were far over expectations, things would soon slow down. In June 1943, women were discouraged, and there was a drop in recruits. The lack of recruits was due to women's unequal benefits compared to men and options for higher pay in jobs outside of civil service. Also, the male-led attitudes that permeated the Army drove women away.

On the first of July, 1943, President Roosevelt signed the legislation, and the WAAC became the Women's Army Corps (WAC), finally incorporated into the U.S. Army.

Once the WAAC became the WAC, the first Women's Army Corps members received their assignments during WWII. Then, after training, they were sent to the Army Air Forces, the Army Service Forces, or the Army Ground Forces. This did not include the Marines. At first, the duties of the WAC performed only a few jobs, but soon, women took on many different duties for the U.S. Army.

As the Navy's manpower began to wane during WWII, the thought of bringing in women, like the WAAC, arose. The bill that would result from a push to bring women into naval service branches was Public Law 689, signed on July 30, 1942. Once signed, it allowed women to join both the Navy and the Marines via the Navy Women's Reserve, called Women Accepted for Volunteer Emergency Service (WAVES) and the Marine Corps Women's Reserve (MCWR). There would also be a women's reserve created in the U.S. Coast Guard during this timeframe, called SPARS.

The reasoning behind the Marine Corps' women's reserve formation was to free up men for combat duty by employing qualified women to serve in on-shore assignments. But, of course, this plan once again would keep women in their places rather than allowing them to join alongside men in offshore combat situations. And in reality, if it weren't for shortages, the U.S. Marine Corps would probably not have formed the women's reserve when it did, since the main point of its formation was to make it easier to move men for on-shore duties to combat.

Although there was some growth since WWI's mistreatment of its Hello Girls, not a lot had changed. The good news is, it was going to.

In the spring of 1943, enemy opposition on Guadalcanal was nil. The American forces had wiped out the enemies, but there was a looming need for more men. If the war continued in the Pacific, the Marine Corps would need to have more troops. This would lead to a big break for women in the U.S. Marines reserve forces.

Once the Marine Corps was in desperate need, the powers at be began incorporating women into jobs that they wouldn't otherwise have held. This entrusting of duties would evolve into women on a more equal playing ground to men, rallying the idea behind its slogan, "Once a Marine, always a Marine." But it would take time for the idea that these women could perform the same jobs just as well as men to truly sink deep.

Throughout the rest of World War II, women Marines held assignments for over "200 different jobs, including radio operator, photographer, parachute rigger, driver, aerial gunnery instructor, cook, baker, quartermaster, control tower operator, motion picture operator, auto mechanic, telegraph operator, cryptographer, laundry operator, post exchange (store) manager, stenographer, and agriculturist" (Molnar, Jr., n.d., para.5). Furthermore, over 85 percent of the U.S. Marine Corps assigned to Headquarters were women at the close of WWII.

One of the most important women in U.S. Marines' history would be Lucille McClarren, the first female Private to enlist as a U.S. Marine.

LUCILLE MCCLARREN: The First Female to Enlist in the MCWR

Lucille McClarren was not only the first female Private in the U.S. Marines, but she was officially the first female to enlist in the U.S. Marines Corps Women's Reserve.

In an article from the Klondike Bulletin from Masontown, Pennsylvania, McClarren's early legacy was already beginning to make headlines. She held the title Private Lucille Ellen McClarren, the first private of the U.S. to join the U.S. MCWR. Lucille was from Nemacolin, Pennsylvania, and the daughter of Mr. and Mrs. Danniel E. McClarren. In 1940, she graduated from Nemacolin grade schools and Cumberland Township High School, Carmichaels in Greene County. Shortly after school, she worked for the U.S. War Department in Washington, D.C., as a stenographer, starting in 1941.

Lucille enlisted in the MCWR on Saturday, February 13, 1943.

She reported for duty in Washington D.C. on a Monday. Lucille had taken a brief visit with her parents before setting off. Standing there as Captain H. W. Branson of the Marine Officer Procurement Unit swore her in was surreal. This meant she was officially a member of the MCWR. She knew active duty was nigh. They were to pay her $50 a month, along with a $200 stipend for her uniforms.

Before she left the war department, her friends at the Army offices threw her a fun sending-off party at the Lotus Club the past December. Now, she was sure she'd be on her way for training at Hunter College in New York.

On Saturday, February 20, the Marine Corps had her as a guest at the Press Building during the Marine Day celebration, and Lucille didn't know what to say. There were no other women there, only men. But everyone was cheering and clapping for her. Someone took her to the front of a large room, and she saw an assembly of high-ranking officers. But, again, they were all men.

Regardless of this, the Public Relations Chief of the Marines, Brigadier General Robert L. Denig, gave her a hearty congratulations.

They asked for a speech. It was like her heart was in her throat, but she stood firm and spoke without really hearing what she was saying. Nonetheless, it came from the heart. "With the Marine band and about 1,600 fighting Marines, press reporters and high officials present, and me, the only girl in the auditorium, you can imagine my excitement and joy," McClarren told them. "I was swamped for autographs and finally had to be escorted from the hall by an honor guard. Little did I expect when I left Nemacolin that one day I would receive all this publicity. But you can tell everyone I'll give my best and endeavor to emulate the brave men in the Marines by doing every assignment given me to the very best of my ability." (*Klondike Bulletin*, 1943, as cited in Harper, 2011, para.11).

McClarren concluded her statement by saying how proud she was: "I am happy and proud to be the first girl Marine private in World War II" (*Klondike Bulletin*, 1943, as cited in Harper, 2011, para.11).

When discussing her aunt, Lucille McClarren, Betty Harper said there was no evidence online much beyond her title as the first enlisted woman Marine. However, McClarren told her niece tales about her time in WWII. McClarren was the model for the first women's Marines uniform. She posed for posters. And she also helped recruit other women alongside the first lady of the United States, Eleanor Roosevelt.

At Hunter College, where she underwent her training, she became the first female drill Sergeant, also noted on her death certificate. During her time at Camp Pendleton, Lucille dispatched soldiers home.

Although Harper says there are gaps in her career history once the war ended, the last career she held was Secretary of the Navy in the Pentagon, working during the Cuban Missile Crisis and the Bay of Pigs Invasion. Sometime during the 1950's or 1960's, McClarren married William Desmarais, a fingerprint analyst for the FBI.

Lucille McClarren's motivation for joining the U.S. Marines isn't public knowledge, but one can imagine during the formation of the MCWR, there was much excitement in the air. Her experience working for the U.S. War Department had already left an indelible mark on her—one that launched her into a career of civil service—but perhaps she wanted more. The chance to work and enlist as the first woman in the MCWR was not only an excellent service to her country but the opportunity of a lifetime.

Even McClarren's niece and family didn't talk much about her time in the war, but it seems she was honored to serve. She looked forward to flinging the doors open so she could rise above her station. After all, she was the first female drill sergeant and the first woman to enlist, and she went on to work in the Pentagon.

REVOKING WOMEN'S Ability to Enlist After WWII

After the atomic bombing of Hiroshima on August 6, 1945, and the subsequent bombing of Nagasaki, Japan on August 9, WWII was drawing to a close. Finally, on September 2, Japan formally surrendered, and U.S. General Douglas MacArthur accepted, putting an end to the Second World War. The end of the war was a great victory for the United States. Finally, the bloodshed was over. But although there had been so much progress concerning women in the armed forces, the U.S. government would take several steps back.

It didn't matter how useful women were in the U.S. Marine Corps in World War II—there was a general idea that they had no place in the service during peacetime. That is precisely what Brigadier General Gerald C. Thomas said in 1945 when he stated his case against active duty female Marines. "The opinion generally held by the Marine Corps is that women have no proper place or function in the regular service in peace-time." Thomas continued to explain his viewpoint, an unsurprising yet considerable bleak assessment of where men thought women should be. "The American tradition is that a woman's place is in the home," said Thomas, before claiming, "Women don't take kindly to military regimentation. During the war, they have accepted the regulations imposed on them, but hereafter the problem of enforcing discipline alone would be a headache" (Stemlow, 1986, p.1).

As with anything concerning women's rights, the idea that these women should be allowed to remain in the Marines was controversial.

Even before World War II ended, women wondered if they could keep their places, while most men were hoping they would go back to mending shirts, cooking, and tending to babies.

The problem, which arose needed addressing—could women remain in the reserve forces? For some of the women who blossomed there, honed their skills, and made a difference, you would think the answer was obvious. But the subject was a complicated one because it would rewrite women's roles in society in America. Although people were split in their opinions, the women reserves (WRs) had done the job, contributing greatly to the war effort, and many saw and acknowledged this fact. They even conceded that in times of severe warfare, such as the world wars, bringing in women to take on wartime duties was necessary. It had happened twice already between the 1910's and the 1940's, so most would assume it would happen again.

However, the truth of the matter was that most Marines, whether they were men or women, did not show much interest in the idea of women remaining in the Marine Corps after WWII was over.

Men's reasoning for this was simple—the Marines was one of the few remaining male-dominated workplaces, so they wanted to keep it that way. However, it's important to remember that it was becoming much more common for women to work in various fields after World War I—at least until they got married. Meanwhile, the senior women officers of the Marine Corps expressed concern for the breed of women they would attract. Even in women's minds during this time, there was this prevalent idea that most 'good" girls belonged in a family setting—the American dream of a husband, a housewife, and the kids. So any woman who would volunteer to join the Marines would, in their beliefs, be of an unusual sort. Perhaps they thought these types of women would be immoral, violent, or sexually atypical during a time when any other relationship besides a heterosexual one was considered to be a sickness.

This is where Colonel Ruth C. Streeter would come in. Streeter was the wartime director of the Marine Corps Women Reserves and believed that the women who would enlist in the Marine Corps outside of wartime would simply be joining to get the benefits, rather than for a passion for serving the United States. Due to these beliefs, Streeter dedicated herself to preventing the Marines from allowing active duty women outside of wartime.

It's interesting to hear when a woman works against women's rights—but Streeter's cause for this was not without some understanding. However, to comprehend her beliefs, one must learn a bit more about the Colonel.

On October 2, 1895, Ruth Cheney Streeter was born in Brookline, Massachusetts. After marrying Thomas Winthrop Streeter in 1917, she moved with him to Morristown, New Jersey, in 1922. As a young woman, she attended Bryn Mawr College, a women's liberal arts college in Bryn Mawr, Pennsylvania. Streeter graduated from Bryn Mawr in 1918. Before the war, she served as a civil volunteer, working in welfare and public health, as well as unemployment relief and elderly assistance programs. At one point in her life, she was even President of the Welfare Board in Morris County, New Jersey. Dedicated to public service, she was also a member of the New Jersey State Relief Counsel, the New Jersey Board of Children's Guardians, and the New Jersey Commission of Inter-state Cooperation.

With that in mind, when WWII began, she was determined to help. Full of patriotism, Streeter felt that he could make a difference in the war, just as she had in her hometown during times of hardship, such as the crippling poverty of the Great Depression.

In 1940, Streeter attended a course in aeronautics at New York University. There, she hoped to learn everything she could about flying. She was interested in planes in the way they moved through the sky like birds. How exhilarating it would be, and how she could lend her service to the war efforts if only they'd have her.

By the time 1941 came, Streeter was the only woman on the Committee on Aviation of the New Jersey Defense Council. From there, she acted as chairman of the Citizens' Committee for Army and Navy, Inc., near her hometown at Fort Dix.

At 46, she earned her commercial pilot's license in 1942. She wanted her pilot's license to join the Navy's WAVES or the Women Airforce Service Pilots (WASPS). Sadly, Streeter would face rejection due to her age, but Streeter was not one to quit.

When Streeter decided she would try the U.S. Marine Corps, she would become the first director of the MCWR. Thus, not only was Streeter the first woman Major of the Marine Corps but she was also promoted to lieutenant colonel in late November 1943 and subsequently to colonel in February 1944.

After WWII, she would resign from the Marines on December 6, 1945. For her dedication and success in initiating the Women's Reserve in the U.S. Marine Corps, Streeter received the Legion of Merit. Her efforts in building the MCWR resulted in 820 officers and 17,640 enlisted women by the end of WWII (Ruth Cheney Streeter, n.d.).

As demobilization procedures for women began after the war, it was mandatory for each woman Marines, including officers and those enlisted, to resign or discharge. The deadline for this demobilization was September 1, 1946.

Women in the Marines 1948 to 1953:

- On June 12, 1948, the Women's Armed Service Integration Act of 1948 made it possible for women to permanently serve in the military fully integrated into the Army, Navy, Marine Corps, and the Air Force. On November 4, 1948, the U.S. Marine Corps officially swore in the first group of Women's Reserve officers. Colonel Katherine A. Towle was sworn in as the first Director of the Women Marines in 1948, shortly after the Integration Act.
- The first eight women enlisted in the MCWR received their swearing-in as official Marines on November 10, 1948.
- Parris Island became the hub for training non-veteran women Marines after integration. On February 28, 1949, Parris Island's 3rd Recruit Battalion at Marine Corps Recruit Depot began welcoming its women Marine recruits, who would officially form the first platoon of 50 women Marines to take their six-week training courses.
- Future Chief Warrant Officer Annie L. Grimes enlisted and reported to boot camp in February 1950. Katherine A. Towle introduced the first evening dress uniform for women

Marines in November 1950. Nine years after the founding of the MCWR, the women Marines (aka "lady leathernecks") attended their first color raising ceremony at the Marine Barracks in Washington, D.C, in 1952.

- Colonel Towle became the first woman line officer to retire from any U.S. military service upon reaching the mandatory retirement age at 55 in 1953. After Towle retired, Lieutenant Colonel Julia E. Hamblet was named the new Director of Women Marines in 1953.
- In 1953, Staff Sergeant Barbara Olive Barnwell was the first woman Marine to earn the Navy and Marine Corps medal for heroism.
- Two more women made history in 1953, Ruth Wood and Lillian Hartley, who became the first women allowed to enter the warrant officer program for the Marines.

5

FEMALE MARINE OFFICER: DISMANTLE OF WOMEN MARINES AFTER WWII

Before the demobilization of the U.S. Marine Corps Women's Reserve, Colonel Streeter asked to be released and resigned on Dec. 6, 1945. Since she felt no women should remain in the MCWR after wartime, she, too, left the service. Although Streeter had accomplished much for the MCWR, she was done, and she would transfer the torch, much to her hope that the Marines wouldn't keep women in service in peacetime. Her assistant, Lieutenant Colonel Katherine A. Towle, became the women's reserve second director of the wartime Marine Corps Women's Reserve. As deserved, she earned a promotion to Colonel.

Although you may think there was not much else to do aside from following through with the demobilization of the MCWR, Colonel Towle took on much responsibility. Not only did she have to oversee the demobilization of the women, but she also had to figure out the postwar solution for a women's organization.

Before she was a colonel and the director of the USMCWR, Katherine Amelia Towle was like any other woman in the early 1900's. Born in Towle, California—an unincorporated community in Placer County, named after her ancestors in the 1850's—on April 30, 1898, education was essential to Katherine as a young woman. She attended the University of California, Berkeley for both her Bachelor's and Master's degrees in political science. First, she graduated with honors in 1920. Then, she worked as an assistant in the Admissions Office and eventually worked in administration at Miss Ransom and Miss Bridges School for Girls. Then, she studied and earned her Master's degree, graduating with flying colors in 1935.

Katherine loved working for the University of California, and felt a sense of pride working in education in any capacity. But when 1943 came, she was working as an assistant to the manager and senior editor at the university's Press, and something came up that made her realize she wanted a change.

She went to her supervisor and requested a leave of absence. WWII was still ongoing, and she heard they were accepting women into the Marine Corps. Although she hadn't thought much of serving in the Corps before, she felt she could grow and succeed in the opportunity. Her supervisor approved the request, and she was off to enlist.

Soon, she was off to serve after accepting her commission, and in February of 1948, the official establishment of the Women's Reserve happened. Her official title was representative for the Women's Recruit Depot in the Bronx.

Katherine excelled quickly in the Marines, but her advancement was no surprise to her. She was a practical, meticulous worker who loved to hash out the details. She was skilled in administrative work and found the tasks exciting, challenging at times, and enriching.

Before Katherine knew it, two years had passed, the war was officially over, and Colonel Streeter had resigned. Suddenly, she was promoted to Colonel and asked to take over the position of director in 1945. She knew the position was a lot to handle, as she worked to demobilize the women Marines, but she could swing it.

Towle had successfully won the hearts of the Marines, with credentials enough to take over the MCWR and oversee the women in the last few legs of their service. However, when the official deactivation of the Women's Reserve happened in 1946, she no longer felt needed, and Katherine went back to work as Assistant Dean of Women at U.C. Berkley. Then something extraordinary happened.

. . .

The Women's Armed Services Integration Act

Because Congress had granted members of the Women's Army Corps (WAC) ongoing status during World War II, the question to make women in service permanent began to circulate in the U.S. Congress again in 1946, the same year that Katherine returned to administrative work. Talks were happening because the previous legislation for the WAC would expire in 1948. Thus, leaders in the Army were the first to request that enlisted women in the WAC be made a permanent part of the U.S. Army, with no more legislation that prevented them from serving or had an expiration date.

It would take two years of legislative debate, but in June 1948, Congress passed the Women's Armed Services Integration Act. Although initially the law was championed by the U.S. Army, the result was an act that granted women the right to serve as permanent members of not only the Army but also the Navy, Marine Corps, and the Air Force.

When representative Margaret Chase Smith of Maine gave a speech to the U.S. House of Representatives on April 6, 1948, she dismissed any of the complicated arguments that came along with debates of women in active service. "[The] issue is simple—either the armed services have a permanent need of women officers and enlisted women, or they do not. If they do, then women must be given a permanent status" (The Women's Armed Services Integration Act, 2019, para. 3). On June 12, 1948, President Truman officially signed the Women's Armed Services Integration Act into public law.

Although Major Hamblet had taken over as Director of the Marine Corps Women's Reserve after Towle left, after the passing of the historic integration act, she recommended Colonel Towle to the post.

At the time, Towle was happy in her position as Assistant Dean but was eventually presented the regular commission by General Clifton B. Cates, the Commandant.

Katherine wasn't sure that she wanted to leave her position as Assistant Dean. She thought of the women whose lives she was impacting, the thrill that education always brought her. But she agreed to General Cates' invitation to meet and discuss the position at the St. Francis Hotel in San Francisco. So finally, Katherine made it to the San Francisco landmark, and it loomed tall above her like a sign of grandeur.

The conversation was pleasant, but Katherine wasn't sure if she would commit. Nonetheless, she enjoyed talking to General Cates and hearing the details. She even voiced her own opinions about what should come with the position, should she take the commission.

After their meeting, Katherine would soon find out she would get her wishes, and the commission was hers.

Following Colonel Towle's acceptance of the position, she would permanently establish the Women's Marine Corps and serve as the first Director of Women Marines after it had become a permanent component. Towles implemented several changes throughout her time as director, including contracting Mainbocher to design new Marines uniforms for the women in 1950 and the first Marine Corps women's evening dress uniform, complete with a red tiara.

Towle knew the real pride of being a woman Marine and worked to represent women who wanted to serve. "The aim of every woman is to be truly integrated into the Corps. She is able and willing to undertake any assignment consonant with Marine Corps needs and is proudest of all that she has no nickname. She is a 'Marine'" (Towle, n.d., as cited in Ermey, 2013).

As the director, Colonel Towle also met Opha May Johnson in 1946, alongside Private, First Class, Muriel Albert. There's a particularly lovely photo of Towle and Johnson standing on either side of Albert, as she's wearing Johnson's old uniform.

After leaving her mark on the Women's Marines, Colonel Towle retired on April 30, 1953. She didn't stop working, though. Instead, Towle returned to serve as the Dean of the Women's office at U.C. Berkeley before being promoted to Dean of Students in 1961.

This extraordinary woman was the first female Dean of Students and significantly impacted creating equality in education. She retired totally from work in 1965 and passed away at 87 on March 2, 1986.

Colonel Towle's voice contributed to the women's cause in the Marines Corps and education. During her years of military service, she earned awards like the Legion of Merit, Navy Commendation Medal, a World War II Victory Medal, and an American Campaign Medal.

. . .

Women in the Marines 1949-1969:

- The first black women Marines enlisted in the Marine Corps in 1949, starting with Annie E. Graham from Michigan. The second black woman to enlist was Ann E. Lamb in New York City.
- Annie E. Graham and Ann E. Lamb reported for boot camp at Parris Island on September 10, 1949.
- The Korean War began on June 25, 1950.
- On July 17, 1953, the Korean War was finally over. Meanwhile, other tensions are brewing, and on November 1, 1955, the Vietnam War begins. On March 2, 1959, Colonel Margaret M. Henderson was named the third Director of Woman Marines. The first woman Marine to receive the promotion to E9 is Master Gunnery Sergeant Geraldine M. Moran in 1960.
- Bertha Peters Billeb became the first woman Marine promoted to Sergeant Major (E-9) in 1961.
- On January 2, 1964, Lieutenant Colonel Barbara J.
- Bishop became the fourth Director of Women Marines. In 1965, the Marine Corps' first woman assigned to attache duty was Staff Sergeant Josephine S. Gebers. She would also become the first woman Marine to receive the Combat Action Ribbon later that year for her experience amid the hostile overthrow of the Dominican Republic government.
- The first Hispanic woman promoted to Chief Warrant Officer is Rose Franco in 1965.
- The first woman Marine to serve in a combat zone in Vietnam is Master Sergeant Barbara Jean Dulinsky in 1967.
- In 1968, Lieutenant Colonel Jenny Wren became the first woman Marine to attend Command and Staff College.

6
CHANGES TO BASIC TRAINING FOR
WOMEN

Before Colonel Towle retired from the Marines, there was another war. This was the Korean War, and the Marine Corps Women's Reserve was again mobilized in August 1950. During the Korean War, the MCWR would reach a total of 2,782 active duty women Marines. Although there had been much advancement, most of these women Marines worked in clerical and administrative positions.

The Korean War broke out in June 1950, when communist North Korea invaded South Korea. At the close of WWII, both the United States and the Union of Soviet Socialist Republics (USSR) had come away as two major world powers. There was a looming threat of war between the U.S. and the USSR, also known as the Cold War anxiety. Since the U.S. Army and Navy were afraid of another war brewing, they partially prompted the integration of women as permanent members of the armed forces through their pressure on Congress.

Beginning in 1949, women Marines began training at South Carolina's Marine Corps Recruit Depot Parris Island. This would usher in another change. A landmark that began to break down both the gender and the racial divide—the first African American women enlisted in the Marines in 1949, one year before the Korean war broke out. And when more African American women enlisted, they weren't segregated, thanks to another integration bill.

Two Boundary-Breaking Women of The Korean War

Annie Neal Graham walked into the enlistment office, grasped the pencil, and filled out her paperwork. She had already passed the physical exam and was ready to make it official. She wanted to be a Marine. She signed the paper that would make her the first African American woman to enlist in the U.S. Marines Corps on September 8, 1949; a brave and remarkable achievement. The Jim Crow Laws were still enforced throughout the country, but because President Harry Truman allowed people of color into the United States Military in 1948, integration was all possible. Annie remembered when he signed Executive Order 9981 on July 26, 1948, and she knew then that she wanted to enlist.

Part of the reason Truman signed the order and pursued allowing African Americans into the armed services without segregation was his revulsion at the recent cruelty. Annie knew and had heard of them. The beatings and murders of African American veterans of World War II. It happened in the South, but everyone had heard of it—the news was everywhere.

Truman himself commented on the barbaric acts. "My stomach turned over when I learned that Negro soldiers, just back from overseas, were being dumped out of Army trucks in Mississippi and beaten," he'd said. But Truman's background was that of a Missouri man, and he'd grown up among the most racist, antiabolitionist beliefs. He would make his stance known during this time—he was turning away from those ignorant beliefs and wanted to fight. "Whatever my inclinations as a native of Missouri might have been, as president, I know this is bad. I shall fight to end evils like this," he said (Evans, 2020, para.8).

Annie wanted to prove herself and prove that she could perform just as well as any man or any white woman. Since the President made it possible, she was encouraged.

Annie got to boot camp for her training and found that boot camp was as tough as she thought it would be. The climate was hot, humid, and the mosquitoes were fierce. Despite the steps toward African American civil rights, the Jim Crow Laws were still hanging in the atmosphere, sometimes with tension you could cut with a knife.

Still, Annie worked hard, sweating and pushing through it all, and graduated boot camp. Now, she was an official Marine. *I feel ready to take on the world*, she thought, so proud of how far she'd come.

Soon, she was sent to the U.S. Marines Corps Headquarters in Washington, D.C. Annie worked in various positions, including the personnel department, special orders, and the publications department.

Through it all, Annie wrote a letter about her experience serving. "I am proud to have been a Marine. It was a pleasure and privilege to serve my country." Annie Graham's daughter, Stephanie Gilliard-Sheard, discussed how her mother's bravery was groundbreaking at the time. "Back then, it was a man's world," said Gilliard-Sheard. "[But] my mother was a patriot. She was proud to have served in the Marines" (Defense Now, 2021).

Also in June 1950, the United States began to strengthen their support of ally France as they battled the Vietnam War against the Viet Minh, a communist threat. But the U.S. would not get involved in the fighting just yet.

Meanwhile, in 1953 there would be another woman Marine with a historic accomplishment. Staff Sergeant Barbara Olive Barnwell became the first female Marine to receive the Navy and Marine Corps medal for heroism.

Barbara was at Camp Lejeune in North Carolina on June 7, 1952. The air was muggy, and Barbara was excited to take a refreshing swim in the Atlantic. She listened to her breathing, paddling her arms above her head, kicking her feet, releasing the tensions of her day. She'd gotten pretty far from the shore and luxuriated in the coolness of the water. Soon, she heard a sound that made her heart sink. Someone was crying for help. Barbara looked in the direction the sound was coming from without wasting time thinking, saw another Marine struggling in the water, heavy surf pulling him down.

She began swimming quickly, rushing to him, for she was no farther than 50 feet away. When she reached him, her lungs were burning, but she grasped tightly to him. He was flinging his arms about, fighting her help, scratching at her skin. Barbara was pulled under the water with him, not once or twice, but a few times as she struggled to get the man to relax. If he would only relax, she could pull him out of danger.

The undertow was so strong, but she knew she could fight it if this man would quit dragging her down underneath the water. Finally, she successfully freed herself from the current, swimming with the man in tow. Her legs were tired, and her arms stung from the pressure of his scratches, but she made it to the shallow end of the water.

A lifeguard, who must have seen the struggle, ran to meet them. "Here, let me help! You could have both died," cried the lifeguard. Soon, both of them were carrying the exhausted man, who'd spent all his strength fighting the current, back to the shore. He had passed out, unconscious. They used a respirator, and he awoke again, opened his eyes, and quietly thanked them both. Barbara had had enough swimming for the day, but she was glad she'd been there to rescue him from danger. She didn't ask for his name. Instead, she walked off to find some other task to undertake, leaving the man in the care of the lifeguard after she knew he'd be okay.

Because of her heroic bravery, putting her own life at risk to save a man from drowning, President Dwight D. Eisenhower awarded her the Navy and Marine Corps Medal in August 1953.

The Civilian Fight for Women's Rights

Women were still fighting for their rights outside of the civil service between the Korean and Vietnam Wars. The Vietnam War wouldn't officially begin until 1955 and it would continue through 1974. Despite the peacetime between these two wars, there was much happening back on American soil in the 1950's and 1960's for women.

One of the women working to make a change was Esther Peterson, who, in 1961, was the director of the Women's Bureau of the Dept. of Labor. Peterson's work would have a serious impact on the future generations of women in America.

Esther Eggertsen, who was born to Danish immigrants in Provo, Utah, in 1906, attended Brigham Young University, earned her degree in physical education in 1927, and went on to get her Master's from Teachers College at Columbia University in 1930. When she moved to New York

City, she met and married Oliver Peterson before moving to Boston, Massachusetts, two years later. In Boston, Esther taught at The Winsor School. Esther had been interested in women's rights earlier and would also volunteer at the Young Women's Club of America (YWCA) during this time.

Although her adult life is as essential as what brought Esther to her place in history, a moment in her adolescence helped shape her direction and beliefs. As a 12-year-old, Esther saw a labor strike as railroad employees fought for eight-hour shifts. The strike occurred in 1918, but there were other labor strikes occurring at railroad companies then, too. One of these was a significantly critical strike that occurred when non-union women workers fought for fair wages after The Cleveland Railway Company hired women conductors, who were offered the same wages as men and a worker's union. Since the Cleveland Conductors' Strikes of 1918 to 1919 also involved women's wage rights and suffrage issues, it would have been even more poignant if young Esther had encountered one of these ongoing strikes.

The strike Esther saw, however, was different. After seeing the angry employees, the young girl concluded that unions were no good, and any labor leader was simply someone who wanted to stir the pot and cause some noise.

Among the other injustices Esther witnessed as an adult was the racial disparity of YWCA. African American women were not allowed there amid the segregation laws, but Esther found this to be against the Y's beliefs. Nevertheless, the organization would eventually integrate women of color, slowly but surely. The first of them was the Phyllis Wheatley Branch in Seattle, Washington.

One moment that got Esther thinking about women's unequal wages was when many of her students at the YWCA were on strike and didn't appear for their regular class. Esther wanted to understand why, so she went to see one of her students, a 16-year-old girl named Eileen.

Esther walked the path to Eileen's home, a squat little place in Boston, with clothes hanging from the second story, drying across a line, and a small door knocker on the front door. She knocked, strictly determined to know why so many of her girls had missed the class at the YWCA. The mother met her at the door and quickly invited her in.

"Sorry for such a mess," said Eileen's mother, who was seated again under the light of a small lightbulb, working on a sewing project.

Esther looked around the room and saw that everyone there was working—including Eileen and her siblings, one of whom was a three-year-old. Eileen smiled at her nervously, but Esther glued her eyes to the toddler counting bobby pins in neat little piles of ten. The other children were placing the counted pins onto pieces of cardboard.

"Sorry, Mrs. Peterson, we've got to work—there's no time to stop, even with company," said Esther's mother, apologetic and embarrassed that they had no tea or coffee to share.

"That's quite all right. Eileen, tell me about this strike."

The girl detailed how it all started, and Esther discovered that the garment company, where the girls from her YWCA classes made housedress for just $1.32 per dozen, had made it even more difficult for them to earn money. Since the workers had to adapt to a sewing change of the pockets, they couldn't make as many dresses as they could before, and therefore, they earned less.

Peterson was appalled and moved to join the girls in their strike, called "The Heartbreakers Strike," the following day. This moment changed Peterson's mind about strikes, and she saw that in numbers, they had the power to prompt a change.

"In the slums, I saw industrial home work, which I'd never seen in my life. I saw the whole thing: everybody had to work, or they didn't eat," Esther told Jewell Fenzi in a December 16, 1992 interview for The Association for Diplomatic Studies and Training Foreign Affairs Oral History Program: Foreign Service Spouse Series. "I just felt, 'I've got to work in the Labor movement, I've got to help alleviate a lot of the [problem],'" said Esther. "So I helped organize that first strike... I got a lot of women to help, and we won, got a new contract. You asked how I got started: that was it" (American Memory, Library of Congress, 2006, para. 69).

The "Heartbreakers Strike" was the turning point for Esther and directed her life toward her labor rights pursuits, including when she joined the International Ladies Garment Workers Union (ILGWU).

Esther spent the 1940's involved with her family life, as well as her role in the Amalgamated Clothing Workers of America. During this time, the couple went abroad for her husband's work, and Esther busied herself by helping to organize the first International School for Working Women.

Then, after years abroad, Esther and her husband came back to the U.S. in 1957. From 1958 to 1961, Peterson worked as a legislative representative for the Industrial Union Department of The American Federation of Labor and Congress of Industrial Organizations AFL-CIO.

Now Esther's story comes to 1961 when she left AFL-CIO to work for President John F. Kennedy as the head of the Women's Bureau in the U.S. Department of Labor. She would also work as Assistant Secretary of Labor for Labor Standards. In her high position, she convinced J.F.K. to assemble the Commission on the Status of Women and also gave her opinion that First Lady Eleanor Roosevelt should be the chair. Since Esther thought it was a government responsibility to address discrimination, she was likely very persuasive when she approached the president with the idea. Thankfully, her vision came to fruition, and she received the honor of executive vice-chairman of the first President's Commission on the Status of Women, a role she held through 1963.

Once established, the commission released a 1963 report that was a prime example of the countless discriminations women faced in nearly every facet of society. The report prompted other state and local governments to create their own women's commissions to study and improve the lives of its women.

Around the same time Esther was working for the President's Commission on the Status of Women, Betty Friedan published a book called _The Feminine Mystique_ in 1963. Friedan's book stemmed from a survey she conducted for her 20-year college reunion. In _The Feminine Mystique_, Friedan's explosive work sheds light on the oppression of middle-class women. Sifting through the limited options available to them, Friedan revealed both the emotional and intellectual aspects of the oppression of women, and it hit home, becoming an instant success. Such a book brought inspiration to the women who read it, including many who felt they needed to search for success outside of the historical role of a contented housewife.

In a place of high esteem, Friedan continued her work for women's rights and co-founded the National Organization for Women (NOW) on June 30, 1966.

In the ensuing tidal wave of people examining women's civil rights, Friedan's influence helped spawn a larger revolution. Under the pressure and uprising growing to expand the civil rights of women and African Americans, President Kennedy made a major move in June 1963—he asked Congress for an inclusive civil rights bill. There were a few reasons Kennedy wanted this, but one of them was the murder of Medgar Evers. Evers was a black civil rights activist who had angered white supremacists rejecting the desegregation of African Americans.

On June 12, 1963, white supremacists assassinated Evers. They shot him in the back of the head in front of his home. The murder occurred shortly after Kennedy made a speech in support of civil rights.

Unfortunately, Kennedy didn't live to see the bill's passage. In November 1963, Lee Harvey Oswald assassinated J.F.K. However, once President Lyndon assumed office, he would finish Kennedy's work, and on July 2, 1964, he signed the 1964 Civil Rights Act into law. At Johnson's side were civil rights leaders like Martin Luther King, Jr., Dorothy Height, and John Lewis.

Title VII of the bill prohibits employment discrimination on the basis of sex, race, religion, and national origin. Thus women would now have more options open to them than ever before.

Once the bill was in effect, the U.S. government established the Equal Employment Opportunity Commission to prevent and punish discriminatory business. After only five years, the commission received "50,000 sex discrimination complaints" (Eisenberg & Ruthsdotter, 1998, para.34). However, the commission did little to address these complaints, and Friedan, along with other chairs of state Commissions on the Status of Women, went on to form the National Organization for Women. Inspired by this group and the NAACP, others founded civil rights organizations for specific groups of women, including business owners, tradeswomen, lesbians, Black, Asian-American, Latinas, and all different sorts of women.

Colleges also embraced women's active roles, where young women got involved in anti-war and civil rights movements. Unfortunately, in these schools, many found that their roles were being overthrown or prevented by men. The men thought leadership roles for these organizations were a man's job, and the women should stick to cooking or other less progressive occupations such as running a mimeograph machine. In response to this ongoing discrimination, young college women started to form their own women's liberation groups to incite changes in their status and society.

There was another massive change on the horizon, and that was combat for women Marines.

WOMEN MARINES in the Vietnam War

The Vietnam War brought about some huge changes for women Marines. Until then, women Marines hadn't seen combat duty. The journey to allowing women on active duty combat wasn't linear, but one can assume it stemmed from the other role changes occurring outside of the military.

Finally, after years of women serving the Military without the option to see action on the battlefield, things were beginning to shift. First, women began entering the Reserve Officers Training Program (ROTC) as early as 1969. Then, in 1975, the Army Chief of Staff approved a consolidation of basic training for men and women after recent test programs proved women could meet every standard but one—the Physical Readiness Training Program.

Since the Marine Corps could curtail a physical training program for the women, by 1977, the U.S. Army policy was a fully integrated basic training for men and women.

The gender gap was slowly closing between 1975 and 1979, as regulations for women altered. For instance, all women were allowed admission to all service academies starting in 1976, thanks to legislation signed by President Gerald Ford. A couple of years later, in 1978, non-combat Navy ships accepted female Marines and sailors.

In the U.S. Army, pregnancy discrimination was a big issue. In August 1973, the Army passed a procedure to discharge men and women who failed to meet mental or physical requirements within 180 days after they enlisted. The discharge regulation included pregnant women. In 1973, the U.S. Army had discharged some 1,034 women due to pregnancy (Morden, 1990).

Similar stories ran through all branches of service, but eventually, the U.S. Defense Secretary eliminated the involuntary discharge of military women due to parenthood or pregnancy.

Soon, there would be the initiation of mandatory defensive weapons training for enlisted women. Women were also authorized for more extended overseas tours, making their terms equal to men, increasing to 36 months from the previous 24-month restriction.

Another landmark was a decrease in the minimum age enlistment for women, effective April 1, 1976. Finally, in October 1979, enlistment qualifications for men and women were the same. As the U.S. Military began to blossom into a more inclusive service in its branches, changes also happened in the Marine Corps.

The Vietnam War marked a landslide in women's civil rights when Master Sergeant Barbara J. Dulinsky was the first woman Marine to report for active combat duty in Vietnam. Landing 30 miles North of Saigon in Bien Hoa, Dulinsky had traveled 18 hours by plane and officially arrived on March 18, 1967. Dulinsky was transported overnight at the airfield there, unable to go by road due to restrictions at night.

After a bus trip and armed escort to Koeppler Compound in Saigon, Dulinsky reported for duty and gave a lecture on security. Her security briefing touched on the threats in Vietnam warfare, including booby traps or other tactics to ensnare members of the American forces, such as cabs with no inside door handles. Barbara Dulinsky's arrival there was not much different from the women Marines to follow in her footsteps.

Barbara J. Dulinsky, born on October 18, 1928, to Ross and Anna Noel Dulinksky, wanted to enlist in the Marine Corps like nothing else she'd ever wanted to do. In 1951, she made her way to the enlistment office and signed up. She would first go to Parris Island in South Carolina before the Vietnam War was underway. It would take some years until women could join men in active duty combat. Meanwhile, Dulinsky served as the Senior Drill Instructor for other female Marines at the Marine Corps Recruit Depot at Parris Island. It took years, but Barbara made up the ranks in the U.S. Marine Corps, eventually receiving the title of Master Sergeant.

In 1967, Barbara knew she wanted to be deployed. She volunteered for deployment to Vietnam, but things were so unequal for women that she didn't expect anything to come of it. The Marine Corps approved her request, and she was blown away. At first, her hands shook for anxious shock, but then she smiled—never had a woman been to an active duty warzone before. She would be the first.

When she began to pack her bags, she was thrilled to seize such an opportunity. Before she knew it, Barbara was on an 18hour flight. When she landed on March 18, 1967, the air was electric, the skies dark, and her excitement ripe. They transported her by aircraft instead of by car, as the roads weren't safe to travel by in darkness. When they landed again, a bus transport took her, along with an armed companion, to ensure there was no trouble along the rest of their journey.

Dulinsky was tired, but she couldn't even tell anymore that she was by the time she gave a security report for other Marines, telling them about the dangers they must be wary of in Vietnam.

After that first assignment, Barbara went on as an Administrative Chief with the Military Assistant Command of Vietnam and served there for a year.

Dulinsky sat to write a letter home, discussing how the transition to an active combat zone was going. "Right now, most of us don't look the picture of 'the New Image.' Whew! Hardly! I can't determine at night if I'm pooped from the workday or from carrying around these anvils tied to my feet called combat boots," she wrote. "Our Young-uns (and me too inside) were scared, but you'd have been proud of them. They turned to in the mess, cashiering, washing dishes, serving and clearing tables," remarked Dulinksky (Barbara J. Dulinsky, n.d., para.2).

Barbara wasn't the only female Marine to serve in Vietnam. A total of 36 women, including Dulinsky, began breaking the gender barriers as they served in Vietnam between 1967 and 1973.

For the women to serve in the active combat zone, life in Vietnam was clearly an adjustment in 1967. After their long journey from the United States, the Marines first sent the women to the Ambassador Hotel for their quarters. Later on, these women would move to the Plaza hotel dormitory, where each woman had a roommate. The women Marines were not the only ones to stay there—the Plaza also housed men and women of other services.

When spring 1968 rolled around, enlisted women Marines would instead stay in the Billings Bachelor Enlisted Quarters (BEQ), near the

U.S. Military Assistance Command, Vietnam (MACV) Headquarters. Women officers were typically placed in Le Qui Don, housing similar to a hotel and used for Bachelor Officers Quarters (BOQ).

Women Marines were often billeted together with the women of the Navy (WAVES). The conditions of these living spaces were not luxurious. Though the women Marines did have air conditioning, the electricity was sporadic, and they didn't usually have an eating facility. As a result, they had to cook in their own rooms, using an electric skillet or a hot plate (when electricity was available). During power outages, they ate charcoal-grilled meals in the dim light; the only prevention from total darkness was their candles.

Their living quarters also didn't offer laundry facilities, so instead, they needed to hire a maid to wash and press their uniforms. The maids also cleaned their rooms for a total of $15 per month.

Before departing, the higher-ups requested the Women Marines bring a plentiful supply of cotton lingerie, nylons, and summer uniforms before deployment because the items were not easy to come by via post exchange (which served male troops more than women). Unfortunately, the maids were also quite rough with these clothing items when they washed these articles of clothing. A prime example of this comes from Lieutenant Colonel Elaine E. Filkins (before she married to become Davies). She said she could see the maid from her window, washing her nylons and lingerie, striking them on rocks in a nearby creek as part of the routine. As you can imagine, this treatment of Filkins' delicates left some of them crumpled and torn.

Any girdles or bras the women had brought with them also had their lives shortened in Vietnam. Nylon stockings were also quite scarce, and the Vietnamese women who encountered them went as far as to touch a Marine woman's legs to feel the smooth material.

Daily life for the Marines serving in Vietnam was in and around Saigon. The weather there would often change at the drop of a hat, so the women needed to wear utilities and oxfords in case of wet, rainy weather, or siege. They also wore combat boots when required.

An event that changed women Marine's experiences in Saigon, and caused quite the upset, was an enemy attack called the Tet Offensive, which occurred in January and February 1968. When enlisted women were staying at the Plaza, an automatic weapons fire broke out. Because of the attack, many of the bus services weren't running, leaving the women stranded. Confined to their quarters, people like Lieutenant Colonel Vera M. Jones waited over a day to go. As you can imagine, it also affected Master Sergeant Dulinsky.

Captain Jones sent a letter to Colonel Bishop, explaining the situation on February 3, 1968. "It's hard to believe that a war is going on around me. I sit here calmly typing this letter and yet can get up, walk to a window, and watch the helicopters making machine gun and rocket strikes in the area of the golf course which is about three blocks away," wrote Jones. "The streets, which are normally crowded with traffic, are virtually bare" (Stremlow, 2000, p.2). Dulinsky also wrote a letter detailing the circumstances on February 9, 1968. "We are still on a 2-hour curfew, with all hands in utilities ... MACV personnel (Women included) were bussed down to Koeppler compound and issued three pair of jungle fatigues and a pair of jungle boots," she wrote (Stremlow, 2000, p. 2).

The Tet Offensive changed their daily lives for a while. However, despite the increased hardships, the women were still able to celebrate the silver anniversary of women in the Marines in a make-shift office party complete with a cake-cutting ceremony. Unfortunately, they could not make it to Okinawa for the full-blown celebration, but their cozy party sufficed to pay homage to the date.

Aside from the obvious intrusion of the Tet Offensive, the women Marines' day-to-day in Vietnam typically included 60hour work weeks, which left the women with little time off. However, when the Marines did enjoy some free time activities, they weren't too varied. In their downtime, they would go bowling, catch a movie in the BEQ or BOQs, or watch American television during the evening. Others devoted themselves to more productive off-time pursuits, such as volunteering at orphanages in need, visiting Vietnamese families, or even working for the Armed Forces Television Station. In addition, Captain Jones had attended a Vietnamese language school and taught English to Vietnamese police officers.

There was a great call to help the Vietnamese orphanages, and many of the American women Marines rallied to help. One of these women was Captain Filkins, who assisted in getting supplies for a blind girls' orphanage, writing to Marine companies back on American soil for help. Meanwhile, Staff Sergeant Ermelina

Salazar's work for Vietnamese orphans would earn her an Unsung Heroine Award in 1970, sponsored by the Veterans of Foreign Wars Auxiliary.

Salazar wrote a letter on September 10, 1969, to Gunnery Sergeant Helen A. Dowd detailing her work for the St. Vincent de Paul orphanage. "I don't remember if I mentioned to you that I had been working with the orphanage supported by MACV. It is not a big one—only 75 children ages from a few weeks old to about 11 or 12 years of age," she wrote. Salazar remarked how lively the children were, despite the lack of resources. The two women in charge of the orphanage were Vietnamese women who spoke no English and "work[ed] themselves to death" (Stremlow, 2000, p. 3). In the letter she also mentioned the severe lack of medical supplies and care.

Salazar organized a Christmas party for the children, receiving contributions for Marine units and taking volunteers to help her make it a reality. Her work didn't end after the holidays, though. Salazar worked 11 hours six days of a week and still found plenty of time to devote to helping the children from the orphanage.

Her dedication earned her a painting by Marine artist Cliff Young and the honor of the Unsung Heroine Award. "Her unusual and untiring efforts to assist these otherwise forgotten children reflect great credit upon herself, the United States Marine Corps, this command, and the United States," wrote her commanding officer, who nominated her for the prestigious award (Stremlow, 2000, p.3).

Another interesting glance into women Marines' experience in Vietnam was how the Corps managed women—and held them back from a proper social life and independence in dating. Suzanne Devlin detailed her experience in the Marine Corps from 1972 to 1975, working as an air traffic controller and a Drill Instructor. Devlin remarked upon the doubt expressed by other family members when she was small and her desire to be employed in a field outside of the typical ones, such as secretarial work or nursing. She tried first to join the U.S. Navy, but when they said they'd call her back, she tried the Marine Corps, who gave her a time quote of 20 minutes for an initial meet-up. "These two guys, probably about 23, 24-years-old showed up in like 30 minutes in dress blues at my house and said, 'How would you like to go out for a spaghetti dinner?'" She signed her enlistment papers right after their dinner.

Devlin remarked that her decision to join the Marines left her on another "sort of battlefield": "I was on another kind of strange battlefield that you don't get any medals for. You shed a lot of blood, sweat, and tears over it—that social battlefield that was America at that time." Devlin continued, "You were sort of managed like property. You know, if any guy wanted to date you, the W. Master Sergeant was watching that, and the men had to sign you out and sign you in."

She continued to explain the attitudes toward women Marines during her service, and they weren't too pretty. "I was told, 'We might have to have you here, but that doesn't mean we have to really want you here.' But again, the Marine Corps motto at that time was to free men to fight. So you have assumed jobs of men, which I was in air traffic control. Only men were in that particular MOS (military occupational specialty code), so I got in flight clearance which was considered unique at the time. A big bust through some of those closed doors."

Another dark side of serving in Vietnam was the ever-persistent gender discrimination and even abuse. "The real turmoil wasn't about the war when you're in the service. The real turmoil was the social fabric of society that was changing that made it a battlefield socially. In fact, I had orders to Okinawa that were canceled because of, essentially, what we'd consider gender wars," said Devlin. "There were women soldiers who were being raped in Okinawa by male soldiers" (The United States of America Vietnam War Commemoration, 2020).

Life in the middle of the Vietnam War wasn't always negative, but it wasn't easy. Other branches of service had a more prominent presence of women serving in the active duty combat zone. Still, the U.S. Marine Corps had only permitted 60 female Marines to serve overseas until 1966, and the Corps sent most of those women to Hawaii. The 28 enlisted Marine women and eight Marine officers to serve in Vietnam from 1967 to 1973 endured long hours, limited free-time activities, sexism in some cases, and comradeship with the other women. Nevertheless, in cases like Devlin's, she came away with leadership skills that would carry through to the rest of her career. Master Sergeant Barbara J. Dulinsky received the honor of being the first woman to serve as a Marine in a combat zone. Meanwhile, Staff Sergeant Salazar spent her days working hard, even in her free time, engaging in humanitarianism and inspiring other Marines to do so.

As with other failures to properly record women's experiences in military services in those years, there isn't a ton of data to reflect the wide variety of women's experiences in the Vietnam War. "The Vietnam Women's Memorial Foundation estimates that approximately 11,000 military women were stationed in Vietnam during the conflict," but many of them were volunteers (History.com Editors, 2011, para.1). Although 90 percent of these women veterans served as nurses, there were female air traffic controllers, clerks, intelligence officers, and even physicians.

Soon, however, the challenges women Marines would face in the modern era would be different, and there would be even more opportunity for them to achieve success in a service branch that was historically closed to them.

WOMEN IN THE MARINES 1970-1990:

- In 1970, 1st Lieutenant Patricia Murphy became the first woman Marine to be certified as a military judge. Chief Warrant Officer Annie Grimes is the first African American to retire from military service with a career that spanned 20 years.
- On August 31, 1972, Lance Corporal Brenda Hockenhull became the first Woman Marine to graduate from the 6-week Test Instrument Repairman Course, finishing as class honor man, which earned her a promotion to corporal.
- Lieutenant Colonel Carolyn Walsh, Commanding Officer of the Women's Officer School, is the first female officer permitted to stay on duty while pregnant in 1972.
- In 1973, Sergeant Major Bertha Billup was the first woman Marine to retire with 30 years of service.

- In 1973, Elizabeth A. Aitel became the first female Marine to join the U.S. Marine band, playing the oboe.
- The first woman named as Commanding Officer of
- Headquarters and Service Battalion, Marine Corps
- Base, Camp Pendleton, Oceanside, CA, is Colonel Mary E. Bane in 1973.
- The first woman Marine tank mechanic, Private First Class Regina T. Musser, was appointed on October 3, 1974.
- Lance Corporal Harriet F. Voisine is the first woman to report for duty as a military policewoman in 1974. In 1974, 2nd Lieutenant Debra J Baughman became the first female officer in the military police field. 1st Lieutenant Catherine A. Kocourek Genovese became the first woman officer to design and teach a course of instruction at the Woman Officer School following its integration into male companies in 1974.
- On April 30, 1975, the Vietnam War ended.
- In 1975, the first female instructor to serve at the Personnel and Administration School in Quantico was Karen Pressler. The same year, 1st Lieutenant Diane S. George was the first woman assigned to the inspectorinstructor staff of an all-reserve men's unit. The first woman Marine to integrate into the all-male security force at Camp Lejeune is 1st Sergeant Margaret Reiber in 1975.
- In 1976, Private Beth Ann Fraser was the first woman Marine allowed to attend the Army Airborne School in Fort Benning, Georgia.
- The first-ever female jet mechanic in the Marines was Private First Class Kate Dixon in 1976.
- The first woman Marine to attend and graduate from the Defense Language Institute was Rhonda LeBrescu Amtower in 1977.
- Other firsts in 1977: Gunnery Sergeant Mary Vaughn is the first African American Warrant Officer, and Nancy Anderson is the first female platoon commander after Quantico's Officer Candidates School fully integrated women.

- The first female general in Marine Corps history was Colonel Margaret A. Brewer in 1978.
- In 1978, Private First Class Myra Jepson became the first woman Marine honor guard at the White House in Washington, D.C.
- In 1980, the U.S. Marine Corps commissioned the first seven female midshipmen from the U.S. Naval Academy.
- In 1985, the first female officers were permitted to possess and train to use a sword.
- The Commandant of the Marines Corps, Alfred Gray, announces all recruits, male and female, are permitted to undergo Basic Warrior Training in 1988. In 1989, Colonel Eileen M. Alberston-Chapman was appointed to the appellate military judge, the first woman to receive the position. That year, Major Doris Daniels also became the first African American woman to earn the rank of Lieutenant Colonel.
- In 1989, Angela Salinas became the first woman Marine to command a recruiting station.
- In 1990, Marie Connie Villescas was deployed to Vietnam and would eventually be the first woman to enter Kuwait's combat zone.

7
A MODERN ERA FOR MILITARY WOMEN

After the WAC was fully integrated into the United States Army, women were able to take on other gender barriers. After the Vietnam War, the U.S. Army got involved in other crises, including natural disasters, more regional conflicts, and various humanitarian issues around the world. As with any new era, the roles of Army women were ever-evolving, and during this time of contingency operations, these strong women faced tests and evolutionary events that would reshape women's place.

Although there are plenty of women who began to break the gender barriers, the first woman to reach the general officer rank in the U.S. Marines is one whose accomplishment is undeniably important. Margaret A. Brewer was this woman, and she began her journey to becoming a Marine straight out of college.

Margaret was born in Durand, Michigan, in 1930. Although she spent her primary years in her hometown, she eventually went to the Catholic High School in Baltimore, Maryland. Young and bright-eyed, Margaret chose to attend the University of Michigan at Ann Arbor and earned a bachelor's degree in geography in January 1952. Just two months later, in March 1952, Margaret was commissioned as a Marine second lieutenant.

Margaret could hardly contain her excitement as she got off the plane in California. Then, finally, she was on her way to El Toro, where she assumed her first assignment as a communications watch officer. The weather was so much warmer there, and her hands were beginning to sweat as she met with the Marine Corps Air Station officers. Soon, they got her settled in, and she was ready to start work.

Margaret loved her work there but would soon move on in June 1953. Her next station was at the Women Reserve Unit in Brooklyn, New York, where she was appointed inspector and instructor.

There was more change in the air in September 1955 when Captain Brewer became Commanding Officer of the Woman

Marine companies at Norfolk, Virginia, and Camp Lejeune, North Carolina. There she found herself in charge of the women Marines, overseeing them, influencing them, and setting examples for them.

Margaret was one for advancement, and any opportunity she had to climb the ranks, she seized. She left her position of commanding officer in June 1958 and then became a platoon commander for women Marine officer candidates in Quantico, Virginia. During the summers, she worked as a woman officer selection officer in the U.S. Marine Headquarters in Lexington, Kentucky, in the off months.

Again, Brewer was on the move in November 1959. During this time, she transferred to Camp Pendleton in California, assuming a role with the Commissioned Officers Mess. She received a notable promotion to major in September 1961 and stayed there in California until April 1963, when she went back to Quantico, Virginia, to take the executive officer position. Later, she would also work as a commanding officer of the Woman Officer School.

In her long career, Brewer also served as the Public Affairs Officer for the 6th Marine Corps District in Atlanta, Georgia, from June 1966 to February 1968. In December of 1966, she received a promotion to lieutenant colonel.

As she continued to advance steadily, Margaret became Deputy Director of Women Marines at Headquarters Marine Corps a month after leaving her position in Georgia. Then, in December 1970, Brewer received yet another promotion—colonel.

Margaret was again called back to Quantico, where she assumed the position of Special Assistant to the Director at the Marine Corps Education Center in 1971. In June 1972, Brewer was named Chief of the Support Department at the Marine Corps Education Center and stayed in this position until February 1, 1973 —the day she was chosen as the 7th Director of Women Marines. Four years later, on July 1, 1977, Colonel Brewer became Deputy Director of the Division of Information at Headquarters Marine Corps due to the integration of women into the Marine Corps. Because women were now fully integrated in U.S. military service branches, there was no need for the Women Marines' office. However, Brewer received recognition for her time in the role, earning the Legion of Merit on June 30, 1977, for her service as Director of Women Marines.

Finally, her career was coming to the ultimate honor in a climatic flash. In April 1978, a higher-up in the Corps nominated Margaret Brewer for an appointment to brigadier general—an honor never before stowed upon a woman Marine. On May 11, 1978, she assumed her title of brigadier general, making another historic stride for women, and began her role as Director of Information.

As the departments changed along with other progressions,

the Division of Information became the Division of Public Affairs on December 1, 1979, and Brewer became the Director of Public Affairs. She worked in this position until she retired from service in 1980. When Brewer passed away on January 2, 2013, the Marine Corps Commandant General James Amos made a statement in her honor, remarking on her contributions to the Marine Corps. "Throughout her three decades of service to our Corps and country, she truly led from the front and helped the Marine Corps integrate women more fully into the force. She served during an era when many thought that women had no place in the Corps, but she proved critics wrong time and again," said Amos. "It's never easy being the first, but she was both the first female general officer and the first Director of Public Affairs and met the challenges and responsibilities of each with professionalism and grace," he concluded in his statement (*Michigan Military and Veterans Hall of Honor, n.d.,* para.3).

During her service, she received two Legion of Merit Medals and also played a hand in creating the National Museum of the Marine Corps.

She also helped establish Arlington, Virginia's Memorial, the Women in Military Service for America Memorial.

Women received more equality in the time Brewer spent her three-decades-long career in the U.S. Marines Corps. One decade after she retired, in 1990, there was trouble brewing, which meant another war. The Persian Gulf War would bring U.S. women into service in large numbers—the largest since women served in World War II. Over 24,000 women would serve in the Persian Gulf War starting in 1990. Otherwise known as Operation Desert Storm (or Desert Shield), the U.S. Army called on its Reserves Forces. There were many enlisted women in the Marine Corps reserves, and the Army would deploy whoever they could. The Gulf War would only last for a short time (from 1990 to 1991), but military leaders agreed that they needed women in the service after it concluded. Prior integration of women throughout WWI and WII, and even in the Vietnam War, the attitudes toward women weren't of entire acceptance. Finally, a significant change was underway concerning the beliefs of women in combat.

Marie Connie Villescas's Tour of Duty

As a woman Marine in the 1980's and 1990's, though times had changed since Opha May Johnson first crossed out the male pronouns and enlisted as the first female Marine, there were still plenty of gender barriers to overcome.

Marie Connie Villescas was 22 when she joined the U.S. Marine Corps in 1982. For Villescas, the decision was an easy one. For as long as she could remember, she wanted to get out of Los Angeles to explore the world and experience other locales. Joining the Marines would ensure that was possible. She'd also seen her sister and her uncle enlist, so by now, enlisting was becoming not only a means of her escape but a family tradition.

Villescas reported for boot camp in January 1983 and was ready to learn. She knew that women weren't going to get the same treatment as men, even though they'd been integrated into the military service since the late 40's. Women could do many jobs in the service, but some roles were still off-limits. Villescas couldn't hold a combat role as a woman, so her basic training was nothing like the simulated combat scenarios men would undergo in their boot camp. She knew this heading in.

A U.S. Marine Corps publication from 1986 outlined some of the boundaries for women Marines, including the physical "limitations." "Women officers receive identical and consolidated training in all areas except where the combat restriction and physiological limitations pertain, i.e., offensive combat, physical fitness training, and sword manual," reads the publication. Further, the booklet elaborated that "participation by women Marines in tactical field training exercises is limited to the defensive role, survival and to support and staff functions on the offense" (Women Marines, 1986, p.3).

There was Villescas, fresh out of boot camp, proud to have completed her training and officially become a U.S. Marine. Her first assignment was in Military Occupational Specialty (MOS): motor transport. Villescas was terribly excited to complete her training at Camp Lejeune in Jacksonville, North Carolina—yet another area she'd never seen. She arrived in North Carolina and thought it exceptionally beautiful, but her main concern was completing her training. The job required her to drive 18-wheeler trucks, a historically male-dominated role. Already, she was doing her part to break down the gender divide, and she was glad of it.

"At that time, 1983, women just didn't drive combat trucks because women weren't allowed in combat," she explained in an oral history interview from March 12, 2007. "But we were the first group to get selected. And there were probably about eight females, and three of us passed" (Harris & Meier, 2018, para.6).

One of the three women who passed, Villescas proudly took her position, driving tractor-trailers around Camp Pendleton in Oceanside, California, for four years. However, during her time there, she faced some frequent doubts from other Marines, who wondered how she could handle the large vehicles when she was only 5'2'. They made comments and jeers, insinuating that she couldn't drive such large trucks at her size, but Villescas knew she'd prove them wrong, and eventually, these men would learn to respect her. "You're just a bunch of old farts, anyway," she would joke in good fun.

During her fifth year in Pendleton, Villescas climbed out of her tractor and retired for the night. The following day, she received the offer for a new position—an instructor in training school. She seized the opportunity and couldn't wait to get started.

Once she completed the school program, Villescas was officially the first-ever women driving instructor to teach U.S. Marines how to operate 16-wheelers.

Soon, though, things would start to change. In 1990, the onset of the Persian Gulf War was official, and to Villescas's surprise, she received deployment orders to Saudi Arabia. "When I got the orders to go, it was like, 'Wow, I'm going to war.' I mean, 'This is real. This is real,'" Villescas remembered.

She recalled the event and how she felt ill-prepared for heading to an active combat zone. "The sad part is, women weren't supposed to go to war up until then, so we were not trained like the women are trained now," said Villescas. "That was the scariest part... I mean, you know, we never went to combat training. So they're shipping us off and didn't send us to combat training even a little bit beforehand. I mean, they just—we went. And that was a concern."

Villescas, though frightened, was ready for the challenge. She still felt ill-at-ease, though, and wondered how things would play out for women who were deployed. "What was I going to see, how was I going to feel, being a female? You know, having our monthly cycle? How was that going to affect us? Affect me?' she asked (Harris & Meier, 2018, para.9-10).

Despite her concerns and the concerns of other military officials and civilians, the women who deployed for active duty made history. After the war was over, the tally of women in the active duty U.S. troops deployed to the Persian Gulf during the Gulf War was about 7% (Gebicke, 1993).

Unfortunately for Villescas, she felt unseen and unheard. During the days leading up to her deployment, she wondered how she would cope without her children and partner. How would they manage? There was no way for her to open up about these concerns, though, because she was terrified they would force her to resign from the Marines. Her partner was a woman, and she identified as a lesbian, which was still not something that the U.S. Marines accepted, and her position was not protected. Being a woman in the Marines was hard enough, but identifying as something outside of the perceived heterosexual norms was worse.

When Villescas recalled her immense stress about her situation and the fear that the Marines would find out her sexual orientation, she said this duality was "like trying to serve your country, yet at the same time, they're trying to get you" (Harris & Meier, 2018, para. 12).

So, Villescas kept her mouth shut and deployed. She arrived in Saudi Arabia in October 1990. In August, Iraq invaded Kuwait, and the operation Villescas now faced was in two parts. The first goal was to set up a camp, which would enable them to work toward the main goal—heading into Kuwait and driving out the Iraqi military and their leader, Saddam Hussein.

Her role in setting up camp included digging holes, constructing outhouses, and setting up Marines' cots. Once December hit, they were only 15 miles away from the Kuwaiti border.

Villescas's day-to-day was a grueling transport, driving fuel and water to the forward elements, each shift on a 24-hour rotation.

Finally, January 15, 1991 came, and thanks to the help of each of the Marines, the 1st Force Service Support Group had successfully transported enough personnel and equipment. This meant the planned airstrike in-theater could commence.

But Villescas's time working toward Operation Desert Storm's official commencement was not without moments of shock. As a woman who was untrained for a combat situation, Villescas worked tirelessly, but she still wasn't desensitized to the sounds of combat. Then, one night, she heard something that chilled her to the bone and filled her with adrenaline. There was suddenly a "percussion of rounds going off," which prompted her to bolt out of bed and gather the other 14 women near her tent. All she had on was sweatpants, but she moved swiftly as they recollected the sound of an aerial bomb. Ever since that scare, she vowed to sleep in her full camouflage uniform and boots.

The bombing sounds during the night would continue once Operation Desert Storm was officially underway. "Life as we knew it went out the door," Villescas remembered. The ground war, called Operation Desert Shield, began in February of 1991. Villescas—used to the sounds of aerial bombs now, but unused to the idea of she, herself, fighting—

was utterly taken aback when her commanding officer came to her in a flurry, telling her she would need to go into Kuwait.

Villescas was very confused and asked her commanding officer if the rules prohibiting women in combat had suddenly changed. The reply was earth-shattering: they hadn't been authorized, but there wasn't anyone else to drive the resupply vehicles into Kuwait. Although one may expect Villescas to refuse this command, she didn't. Instead, she asked her commanding officer to document everything concerning her and the other women's drive into Kuwait. She also asked for the documentation to include the knowledge that they undertook their actions despite the rules prohibiting it.

Her commanding officer was also a woman and understood her request entirely, agreeing to take down the actions in writing.

"Talk about a milestone. You talk about a milestone of female tractor-trailer drivers taking a forward unit, a general and his whole element, into combat, was huge. Not to mention the fact that I started my period. I was under such stress," said Villescas. "And I'm saying this also on camera because at the time, legislation, Congress, whoever—they didn't want females in war, because of—that was one of the big reasons."

Villescas recalled the inconvenience of the situation, saying, "What's a female to do without—there's no outhouses there. We were driving through minefields, okay. You couldn't just pull a vehicle over and just—even use the bathroom in the sand because we were surrounded by minefields."

Remembering how utterly stressful the situation was, Villescas adds, "So I was able to wait until we actually stopped as a unit. And my truck, thank goodness, was a very large 18-wheeler like I said." She continued, "I was able to get two of my favorite young lance corporals that stuck by me the entire time. Modesty goes out in war. I said, 'Look, bottom line is, I'm on my period. I need to change. I'm surrounded by men, and I can't go outside of this little trail that we're on because we're surrounded by minefields. I need one of you to stand here and one of you to stand here, and you're going to keep everybody away within ten feet of this truck.'"

The women had her back, and Villescas got under the truck and came back out successfully.

"And that's one way for females... So when they say that a female can't go to war—where there's a will, there's a way, and when there's a need, you're going to find a way. Again, another milestone crossed, I guess," said Villescas (Harris & Meier, 2018, para. 19-28).

Villescas was there for the completion of Operation Desert Shield and spent another three months in Saudi Arabia with the Marines, tearing down their tent city. Finally, she made it home safe and was there for four months before the Marine Corps deployed her to Iwakuni, Japan. Villescas would spend a year in Japan but knew soon after the Marine Corps redeployed her that she couldn't stay in the Marines. The shock of entering into an active combat situation had shaken her, and she needed time to process. Unfortunately, another deployment meant she would be leaving her family again, and eventually, this realization ended her relationship. Villescas left the Marines in 1994 after completing her tour in 1993.

Angela Salinas: The First Female Major General

When Angela Salinas was born in Alice, a small city of Texas, on December 6, 1953, her parents had no idea their youngest child would be one of the most boundary-breaking women in the U.S. Marines' recent history. From a proud Texan background, Salinas' native Texan parents came from a lineage that included one of the first civilian settlers in Texas.

Before making Marines history, Salinas received a Bachelor's Degree in History from the Dominican University of California. Later, she would earn a master's degree from the Naval War College.

The reason Salinas joined the Marines was a chance encounter. On April 30, 1974, Salinas, carrying a letter to mail it, was stopped on her way to the post office by a Marine. This man asked her a simple question: "Why aren't you a United States Marine?" When she tried to get away and go about her day, he continued to speak. "You're joining an institution that right now doesn't really want women," he began. "But I will tell you; you will earn everything that you'll get" (Davis, 2015, paras.13-15).

Only a few days later, Salinas went to enlist. On a gorgeous spring day on May 4, 1974, when Salinas enlisted in the U.S. Marines Corps. Only days later, she found herself at boot camp at Parris Island, South

Carolina. When she enlisted, there were fewer than 2,000 women enlistees (Davis, 2015).

Her first position was as a legal services clerk at Marine Corps Base Camp Pendleton in Oceanside, California, and the Marine Air Reserve Training Detachment in Alameda, California. When Salinas detailed her experience at boot camp, remarking that modern-day boot camps were so different. First of all, boot camp was segregated, and female Marines were still not allowed to engage in active combat roles. "You know, we were taught makeup and how to do your hair. And, you know, that was kind of expected because that was the face of a woman Marine," Salinas said in an interview for the PBS documentary series, "Makers." By 1974, however, it became clear that women could be more than just a pretty face. "Women are starting to demand to be recognized as a valuable resource for the nation," Salinas said of the era (*Makers: Women in War*, qtd. in SCPR 2014).

She would work in her legal services position and an inspector-instructor staff member for the 4th Reconnaissance Battalion in San Antonio, Texas, until 1977. But Salinas' journey into the Marine Corps had more than one boundary-breaking effect—yes, she was a woman, but she was also a Latina woman. "I knew, looking around, there weren't [Marines] who looked like me," she says. "But, it wasn't until years later that being a Latina as well meant so much" (Moreno, 2016, para.2).

After spending those three years in her other positions, the Marines Corps selected Salinas for the Enlisted Commissioning Program in 1977. By December 1977, the U.S. Marine Corps commissioned her as a Second Lieutenant.

When she went to an officer training camp, Salinas said there was no gender segregation, and there were no differences in how the women and men were trained, except for different physical fitness tests. "These were like baby steps for the United States Marine Corps as they were trying... how best to [utilize] this untapped resource that was now beginning to flood the gates," she recalled (*Makers: Women in War*, qtd. in SCPR 2014).

After officer training, Salinas was assigned to the Second Marine Aircraft Wing at MCAS Cherry Point in Havelock, North Carolina, where she served as the legal services officer. A couple of years later, she was assigned to Women Recruit Training Command in Parris Island and headed back to South Carolina. She would serve in a few vital roles, including as a series commander, an executive officer, and eventually, a battalion operations officer.

Salinas's ever-storied career would not stop there. In 1986, she served as command of Headquarters and Service Company, 1st Maintenance Battalion at Camp Pendleton. A year later, in 1987, she was named deputy G-1, 1st Force Service Support Group at the same base.

Salinas would transfer to Charleston, North Carolina, the following year to assume the executive officer role for Recruiting Station Charleston, where she would also serve as commander a year later. Finally, another first came in June 1989—Salinas was promoted to command of Recruiting Station Charleston, making her the first woman Marine in charge of commanding a recruiting station. Her service in this role was also during the threat of the impending Gulf War tension.

Her career advancement would continue to break records for female Marines. In June 1992, Salinas began working as a Combat Service Support Ground Monitor for the Manpower Management and Officer Assignments at the Marine Corps Headquarters in Washington, D.C. Assuming this role was a considerable responsibility, Salinas was now in charge of 1,000 senior officers' assignments.

"As I became more senior in my career, I found more young people kind of being drawn to me," Salinas said in a 2016 interview with San Antonio Magazine. "It was kind of this gradual transformation for me personally. I always just wanted to be a good Marine. Not a good woman Marine, not a good Hispanic Marine. Just a good Marine. As I matured professionally, I kind of recognized the responsibility I had" (Moreno, 2016, para. 3).

When Salinas became a Deputy, a Special Assistant for General/Flag Officer Matters at the Office of the Director, Joint Staff at the Pentagon in Arlington, Virginia, in 1993, onlookers probably knew she would keep progressing up the ranks. Three years later, Salinas moved again to Parris Island, commanding the 4th Recruit Training Battalion.

Salinas then took on the role of Assistant Chief of Staff, G-5, for III Marine Expeditionary Force, in Okinawa, Japan, in 1999. However, another milestone was right around the corner. In May 2001, Salinas became the first woman to serve as a Recruiting District Commanding Officer for the 12th Marine Corps District.

Her next great record-breaking position was even closer now. First, she worked as Chief of Staff at the Marine Corps Recruiting Command at Quantico from 2004 to 2006, and then she would be well on her way to the most important promotion of her life—one that a woman had never had before.

After her years of service, Salinas found herself promoted to the rank of brigadier general on August 2, 2006. Two days later, Salinas assumed command of San Diego, California's Marine Corps Recruit Depot/Western Recruiting Region. In August 2009, she would transfer to the manpower management of Manpower and Reserve Affairs at Marine Corps Base Quantico.

Less than a year after her transfer to Quantico, Salinas was selected for a promotion to Major General in March 2010. On May 12, 2010, the U.S. Marines Corps officially promoted Salinas, making her the first woman to become a Major General.

During Salinas's 39-year career of military service, she made not one but several records. Her first record was becoming the first of her family to graduate from college, followed by becoming the first Latina to serve as a general officer and the first woman to command the Marine Corps Recruit Depot.

In 2013, U.S. Marine Corps Major General Angela Salinas retired from service. In her retirement, she found a new role working as chief executive officer of the Girl Scouts of Southwest Texas, where she hopes to instill in the girls a sense of leadership and success.

Remembering the Marine Corps Recruit Depot in San Diego, California, Salinas said she "envisioned that these women would be a cut above" but found that the recruits were people who didn't get the care they needed at a young age. "They were kids that were escaping," she said.

"I used to stand there and think, 'If there was some way to get to these kids when they were younger, instead of waiting until they're 18, imagine how successful they could be,'" Salinas continued (Robinette, 2019, paras.9-10). Salinas, despite her retirement, is continuing to push the gender barriers and inspire young girls to be women of great success.

Women in the Marines 1991 to 2009:

- Colonel Eileen M. Albertson-Chapman is the first woman to lead the Naval Clemency and Parole system in 1991, before heading the Navy disability system in 1992.
- In 1992, Angela Salinas was the first woman assigned as combat service support ground monitor.
- In 1993, The Secretary of Defense, Les Aspen, tossed out outdated restrictions and permitted women in the military to fly in combat aircraft.
- The first African American woman Marine Colonel is Gilda Jackson in 1995, who also was the first woman to command Cherry Point's Naval Aviation Depot. In 1996, The first woman three-star officer in the U.S. Armed Forces was the Marine Corps Lieutenant General Carol Mutter.
- The first female Marine striker fighter pilot earned wings of gold in October 1997, one Karen Fuller Brannen.
- In 1997, the first group of male and female integrated Marines completed their Marine Combat Training Course at Camp Geiger in North Carolina. In 2001, Colonel Angela Salinas again made history when she became the first woman to be appointed as a recruiting district commanding officer. Captain Vernice Armour made waves as the first African American pilot of any gender in 2001 before becoming the first black woman to combat pilot with combat missions in Iraq.
- In August 2006, Angela Salinas was named the first woman Marine to command the San Diego Marine Corps Recruit Depot after breaking the mold as the first female Hispanic brigadier general in the Marines. In 2009, the first all-female Marine team conducted its first mission in Southern Afghanistan.

8

WOMEN'S RIGHTS: THE FIGHT CONTINUES

The stories of women Marines are varied and powerful, but the common thread between them is the lack of justice, freedom, and civil rights. Although society has come far, there is still a way to go before America—and the U.S. Marines—can call women truly equal to men in the eyes of the law.

Since the Seneca Falls Convention of 1848, there have indeed been many improvements to the situation of women. The topics discussed during that history two-day event have, and were, for the most part, resolved. Women can now vote, they can own property, and they are not beholden to their husbands. In those senses, they are free. But there are other issues the modern Women's Rights Movement from the 1990's and beyond addresses that the ladies of the Seneca Falls Convention would never have imagined writing into the Declaration of Sentiments. These current issues are often beyond the question of equal rights, with some considered controversial, even between different groups of feminists.

Many topics are seemingly bipartisan issues—Republicans tend to take the stance against these feminist concerns while Democrats champion them. However, it goes beyond politics for most women. In the opinion of many, it should not even concern the government outside of legislation that would endow the freedoms they seek.

The first of these issues the Women's Rights Movement continues to fight is probably the most controversial of women's reproductive rights. Even 25 years after the United States Supreme Court ruled in favor of reproductive concerns in the landmark case Roe v. Wade (at the helm of which was the late Justice Ruth Bader Ginsburg), the questions concerning reproductive rights and pregnancy termination are still a hot-ticket debate. Roe v. Wade may have affirmed women's choice for the first two trimesters, but there are plenty of states, organizations, and politicians who would change this if they could and strive to prevent women's choice in nearly all areas. There has, in recent years, even been a general attack on women's birth control access. An example of this was the U.S. Supreme Court case decision in Burwell v. Hobby Lobby on June 30, 2014, which allowed certain employers to prevent employees' access to birth control. According to Planned Parenthood, the decision impacted more than half of all workers in the U.S, which is "tens of millions of workers at companies in which five or fewer people own more than 50%" (Planned Parenthood Action Fund, 2014, para.1).

In 1975, President Gerald Ford signed Public Law 96-106, which finally made it possible for women to attend military academies as students. The portion that directly mentions women reads as follows: "Such authority must be exercised within a program providing for the orderly and expeditious admission of women to the academies, consistent with the needs of the services, with the implementation of such program upon enactment of this Act" (Public Law 94—106, 1975). The following summer, military academies began admitting women.

One such example was the first new women cadets to the U.S. Military Academy on July 7, 1976. Among the women to join military academies in 1976 were 119 enrolled at West Point, 157 admitted to the U.S. Air Force Academy, and 81 entering the U.S. Naval Academy (Silva, n.d.). As women were attending military academies, they were also beginning their service in active combat roles. Of course, this is yet another issue that modern feminist movements are continuing to fight for. Some people don't know that women in combat are desirable and would rather not see them on the battlefield. It's a controversial take when the same people who champion freedom and equality for women begin to question whether the war front is "a proper place" for women.

However, many veterans are full of pride in their service and only want women to continue to advance, receiving higher positions and representing a higher percentage of personnel. One of these women fighting the gender gap, whose experience in the U.S. Naval Academy was a mixture of emotions, expressing the attitudes directed toward her when she first arrived in Annapolis, Maryland, in 1976.

Janie L. Mines called the atmosphere upon stepping foot into the academy "mutually exacerbating for everyone who was there." Mines continued, detailing her feelings about her experience, "The academy wasn't ready for [women]," she said. "It just happened quickly, and it needed to be done. The academy considered itself to be a combat school, and [women] were not allowed to serve in combat," she explained (Cronk, 2020, paras. 1-2).

Mine says the men there were pretty hostile about it, recalling, "We were seen as taking up spots for good combat officers that were needed because we 'couldn't do the job.' Additionally, there was a general belief that as Black women ... I would not be able to lead in what was at that time a white-male Navy" (Cronk, 2020, paras. 1-2).

Despite the uncomfortable energy, Mines became a Navy lieutenant in the support corps. She also held the title of one of the first women in service on a Navy ship. Lieutenant Mine also made history as an African American woman. "When the academy called and said I would be the only Black woman who would be admitted, I felt it was something I had to do" (Cronk, 2020, para.10). Successes like Mine's, however, are still being argued in feminist and anti-feminist groups today—should women be allowed at military academies? Should they be allowed in active combat? Whatever the attitudes, the law says they should.

Another topic of dispute? Women who hold a leadership role in a religious sect, congregation, or similar position. Most feminists champion women in high-authority roles in all careers, including those in religion—but some religious sects still discriminate. Even now, there aren't very many women represented in such positions compared to men.

As David Crary of AP News reports, "Women in several faiths are still barred from ordination. Some are banned from praying alongside men and forbidden from stepping foot in some houses of worship altogether. Their attire, from headwear down to the length of their skirts in church, is often restricted" (2019, para. 2). Meanwhile, a Pew Research Study from March 2016 suggests that even though many of America's religious institutions are open to receiving women in leadership positions, very few women have served in the top positions in modern U.S. history (Sandstrom, 2016).

Among the most restricted religious sects to allow women to expand to the top positions are Orthodox Judaism, conservative Hindu branches, Islam, and Christianity. All of these religions also have something in common: Translations of their holy texts have, for years, justified the exclusion of women in favor of a male hierarchy. In addition, one of the most powerful religious authorities recently showed its attitudes toward women are changing and how poorly the churches are handling it. The promotion of a woman to one of the top roles in the Vatican as a manager in the Secretariat of State, courtesy of Pope Francis in January 2020, was done in response to pressure from women's rights activists. Still, Celia Viggo Wexler, author of *Catholic Women Confront Their Church*, pointed out that women are still very much discriminated against in the Vatican: "Not only are women barred from ordination to the priesthood, they are not even allowed to vote at Vatican synods, convened to advise the pope about challenges facing the church" (2020, para.2).

Other issues modern-day feminists continue to battle include affirmative action and the question of whether women face an equal field now against their male counterparts. Should there be further reparations for the discrimination women have endured in U.S. and world history? Are these current compromises, acts, laws, inclusions, and so-called equality moves appropriate enough?

What about women's familial responsibilities? Many women who choose to have children certainly ask for businesses to reasonably accommodate them on maternity leave. There's also a recent call for making child care free and included in America's unionized businesses, especially for communities that face more significant disparities. Most feminists champion a workforce where a woman's job is equal to men's, but things are more complex when bringing up the issue of children and family. One side asks that a woman receive accommodation from their workplace to balance her career and family. The other side argues that the law should not undertake an accommodation that would jeopardize their opportunities for advancement.

Then, there's the ever-prevalent argument of pornography and sex workers. Is pornography a male-dominated institution that demeans and degrades women, or is this now an issue of free speech? Are today's sex workers women who deserve respect, value, and the credibility of other professionals, especially with the recent surge of social media sex workers who choose this for themselves, including those on Only Fans?

Next is sexual harassment, a much-maligned issue from men who don't seem to understand the proper boundaries. In the #MeToo era, what is harassment? When does innocent flirting become something highly inappropriate? As women, one feels invariably certain about what constitutes a sexual harassment claim—if it makes you feel uncomfortable, violated, or anything negative and should not be a part of the workplace, it is sexual harassment.

Others question surrogate motherhood as a civil right— usually, the same who question women's reproductive rights as a whole. Is it appropriate? Does this woman have the right over her own body, the choice to carry another family's child? Is this, and should this be, an unrestricted right for women who wish to make a business of reproduction for women who cannot bear children?

Meanwhile, are Social Security benefits equally and adequately allocated? Do stay-at-home women who suddenly become widows receive enough money to prevent them from poverty? Are these earnings equal to a widowed working woman?

These issues are among the many tackled by young feminists in our modern times, who call themselves "the third wave." There is even a debate among feminists and social researchers that "the fourth wave" has already begun. But, if it has not, is it soon on the way?

Many women are still hesitant to label themselves as "feminists" since the movements have been followed by a backlash, even from some fellow women. Although this is true, these same women would likely not trade the long list of personal freedoms, opportunities, and civil rights that feminist waves have championed for and won over 150 years of America's history. Although each woman may envision something different for their own life, when it comes to the lives of their daughters, granddaughters, nieces, and the many generations to come, things are slightly different. Isn't opportunity and an equal world where these girls can grow and develop freely to take on their dreams what each woman wants?

The women of our modern era live the legacy of seven generations of women who first began and continued advocating for women's rights. These women put their blood, sweat, and tears into a movement that they believed in to free future generations of women and themselves from the bondage of society.

Alice Paul, the advocate and organizer who underwent starvation protests, jail time, and personal deprivation to fight for women's equality, said, "I always feel the movement is sort of a mosaic. Each of us puts in one little stone, and then you get a great mosaic at the end," (Eisenberg & Ruthsdotter, 1998, para. 52). But, unfortunately, her Equal Rights Amendment has yet to come to fruition as an official amendment to the U.S. Constitution.

Although the U.S. Senate and the House of Representatives passed the amendment in 1972, there were never enough states to ratify it to make it official. The time limit for ratification was seven years, but when the deadline of June 30, 1982, came, there were only 35 ratifications.

It's clear, however, that women have advanced far above where they were over a century ago. As women have continued to work on this grand mosaic, each adding their own piece, women's rights have expanded against seemingly impossible odds. Each woman offering their own contribution should remain proud of the legacy of women, rising from a position of powerlessness to a more equal ground. It has been 173 years since the foundation of the Women's Rights Movement, and the progress since that first beginning is genuinely incredible.

WOMEN IN THE MARINES 2010-2021:

- In 2011, Brigadier General Lori Reynolds was the first female Marine Commanding General of the Marine Corps Recruit Depot at Parris Island, Eastern Recruiting Region, and served until 2013. Also in 2011, The Marine Corps selected the first

woman Marine to take the role of Marine Corps Base Sergeant Major of Quantico, Virginia, Sergeant Major Laura Brown.
- Shalanda Raynor became the first female Marine to achieve the rank of Master Gunnery Sergeant in her specialized role as chief of Combat Camera in 2012. In 2012, the first group of women Marines took the Combat Leadership Test.
- Corporal Cheriess Page is selected as one of the first women to receive official orders to the Marine Corps Logistics Base in Barstow, California, a unit that was previously restricted to infantrymen only. In June 2013, a Marine Corps Lieutenant Colonel, Nicole A. Mann, was appointed as one of eight members of NASA's 21st NASA astronaut class. In July 2015, she completed her Astronaut Candidate training, awaiting future assignments.
- Three women Marines, PFC Julia Carroll, PFC Katie
- Gorz, and PFC Christina Fuentes Montenegro,
- graduated from the Marine Corps' enlisted infantry training course in 2013.
- In 2014, Brigadier General Helen Pratt was selected as the first woman President of the Marine Corps University.
- In 2016, the first women Marine Officers and Drill
- Instructors received a permanent assignment to Marine Corps Recruiting Depot, San Diego, Western Recruiting Region, to work with male Battalions. In 2017, the first female Marine PFC, Maria Daum, joined the infantry via its traditional training. Meanwhile, Gunnery Sergeant Stacie Crowther becomes the first woman Assistant Drum Major for The President's Own United States Marine Band.
- Also, in 2017, the first female Marines graduate from the Marine Corps Infantry Officer Course and the Amphibian Assault Officer School.
- In March 2018, the first gender-integrated Marine Combat Training company was ready for business on the West Coast.
- April 2018, Colonel Lorna M. Mahlock becomes the first

African American female to receive the promotion to the rank of brigadier general.
- In August 2018, the first woman Marine led an infantry platoon, Lieutenant Marina A. Hierl.
- On March 11, 2019, Captain Anneliese Satz became the first Marine Corps woman to pilot an F-35. On June 17, 2019, Lance Corporal Megan Browning was named the first female singer in the vocalist MOS role. In February 2020, Chief Warrant Officer Karen Dymora became the first woman commanding officer of a Marine Corps correctional facility, taking charge of the Camp Pendleton Brig.
- In June 2020, Lieutenant Colonel Juliet H. Calvin assumed command of the Marine Corps Network Battalion, the first woman to command this type of unit.
- On August 18, Captain Shaneka Shaw became the first
- Black woman Marine to receive the qualification to fly MQ-9 Reapers.
- On December 16, 2020, the Marine Corps Recruit Depot, San Diego, graduated its first female Marines from its Drill Instructor School.
- In February 2021, the first female Marine recruits in San Diego took on and passed "The Crucible".

AFTERWORD

For years women have fought for their place in the U.S. Marines Corps, demanding acceptance and equality. However, these battles began in the mid-1800's, long before women could legally join the Marines. When Elizabeth Cady Stanton first gathered with her friends at tea time and formulated a plan for the first Women's Rights Convention, the first question of whether an expansion of women's roles was possible arose. Despite the decades chipping away at resolutions for Stanton's issues listed in the Declaration of Sentiments, there is a third wave of feminism that is still duking it out, fighting for an expansion of women's rights so there is finally a true equality realized.

The inspiring women who made it possible for females to enlist in the Marines began with Opha May Johnson when she first scratched out the male pronouns on her enlistment sheet, but they did not end with her. Other women like Alice Paul, Lucy Burns, and the Silent Sentinels took to the streets and argued for women's suffrage, a step which was a personal sacrifice for them, resulting in imprisonment and abuse. However, the step was a necessary one to secure women's place in the military years later. Because of these sacrifices, the passage of the 19th Amendment on August 18, 1920 came to fruition.

Once women secured the right to vote, there was still more work to be done. From Margaret Sanger's call for women's reproductive rights to Lucille McClarren, the first woman to officially enlist as a U.S. Marine after the formation of the MCWR, change was in the air. The fights these women undertook paved the way for other Marine Corps firsts. These firsts included Ruth Cheney Streeter's dedication to the MCWR as its first director, despite her controversial belief that women had no right to continue in the Marines after WWII. The list is full of names—Lieutenant Colonel Katherine A. Towle's further development of MCWR as the second director, Annie Neal Graham, the first black woman to serve as a U.S. Marine, and the overlooked women who've taken small steps for womankind, devoting their lives to service to make it all possible.

The many achievements of women who laid the groundwork for females in the Marines did not stop. For example, Staff Sergeant Barbara Olive Barnwell became the first female Marine to receive the Navy and Marine Corps medal for heroism in 1953 when she saved a male Marine from drowning. In civilian efforts, Esther Peterson convinced Kennedy to create the Commission on the Status of Women. In addition, Betty Friedan's ground-breaking 1963 book, *The Feminine Mystique*, brought many women to the forefront of women's rights.

Finally, in 1967, Master Sergeant Barbara J. Dulinsky made another women's first in the Marines as the first woman to report for active combat duty in Vietnam. Among these women who worked in the active combat zone was Staff Sergeant Ermelina Salazar, the woman who valiantly cared for Vietnamese orphans, a dedication that earned her the Unsung Heroine Award in 1970. Soon, in 1978, Margaret A. Brewer became the first woman Marine to reach a general officer rank as a brigadier general. By the time the Gulf War of the 1990's began, women had overcome many obstacles, but they were still not allowed to engage in combat duty. However, the Marine Corps deployed Marie Connie Villescas to Saudi Arabia in 1990. She would deliver supplies into the active combat zone, becoming the first woman (despite its prohibition at the time) to engage in combat duty (though she fired no weapons) in Kuwait.

In 2010, Angela Salinas became the first woman Marine to receive the rank of Major General.

All of these storied achievements added stones to Alice Paul's proclaimed mural of women's advancement. Yet, although the U.S. Marines Corps has come far from the days of Opha May Johnson, there is still much work to be done. Women are still fighting for other rights that have yet to be addressed, including representation in religious positions, equal access to birth control of all kinds, further representation in the Marine Corps and other military branches, affirmative actions, cooperation with women's familial life in the workplace without hindering advancement, protections against sexual harassment, equality in Social Security benefits, and more.

As women continue to live their journey, it's important to remember that the legacy you live on is one of the generations of women who fought for Marine Corps representation, suffrage, and the often undervalued fundamental civil rights of the modern-day. Every woman has a role in advancing equal rights at every level, and how you choose to fight your battles and the battles of women everywhere is your choice. Whether you are thinking about enlisting in the U.S. Marine Corps, are already a Marine, or are simply studying women's history in the Marines, it's a hope that you'll come away with the desire to fight for equality, too, as women's rights are still not accomplished.

Assuming a leadership role as a woman is one step that makes a difference, and there are many other ways to climb your way up the ranks and prove that equality is an issue worth fighting for.

REFERENCES

The American Federation of Labor and Congress of Industrial Organizations (AFL-CIO). (n.d.). Esther Eggertsen Peterson | AFLCIO. Aflcio.org; The American Federation of Labor and Congress of Industrial Organizations (AFL-CIO). https://aflcio.org/about/history/labor-history-people/esther-peterson

American Memory, Library of Congress. (2006). *Interview with Esther Peterson*. Tile.loc.gov; Library of Congress, The Foreign Affairs Oral History Collection of the Association for Diplomatic Studies and Training. https://tile.loc.gov/storage-services/service/mss/mfdip/2004/2004pet02/2004pet02.xml

Angela Salinas, Major General, U.S. Marine Corps. (2020, April 18). Foundation for Women Warriors; Foundation for Women Warriors. https://foundationforwomenwarriors.org/angelasalinas-major-general-u-s-marine-corps/

Army Women's Foundation. (n.d.). Army Women in History –Army Women's Foundation. Armywomensfoundation.org; Army Women's Foundation. https://www.awfdn.org/army-women-inhistory/#1900

Barbara Barnwell - Recipient -. (n.d.). Valor.militarytimes.com. https://valor.militarytimes.com/hero/41550

Barbara Dulinsky, Master Sergeant, U.S. Marine Corps. (2020, April 22).

Foundation for Women Warriors; Foundation for Women Warriors. https://foundationforwomenwarriors.org/barbaradulinsky-master-sergeant-u-s-marine-corps/

Barbara J. Dulinsky. (n.d.). The Legacy of Women Marines. https://womenmarinecorps.weebly.com/barbara-j-dulinsky.html

Brigadier General Margaret A. Brewer. (n.d.). Www.usmcu.edu; United States Marine Corps University. https://www.usmcu.edu/Research/Marine-Corps-History-Division/People/Whos-Who-inMarine-Corps-History/Abrell-Cushman/Brigadier-GeneralMargaret-A-Brewer/

Burnette, B. R. (2009). *Comstock Act of 1873.* Mtsu.edu; Middle Tennessee State University. https://www.mtsu.edu/firstamendment/article/1038/comstock-act-of-1873

Cengage. (n.d.). *Streeter, Ruth Cheney (1895–1990) | Encyclopedia.com.* Www.encyclopedia.com; Cengage. https://www.encyclopedia.com/women/encyclopedias-almanacs-transcripts-and-maps/streeterruth-cheney-1895-1990

Civil Rights Act of 1964 (U.S. National Park Service). (2017). Nps.gov; National Park Service. https://www.nps.gov/articles/civil-rightsact.htm

Colonel Barbara Janet Bishop. (n.d.). Www.usmcu.edu; United States Marine Corps University. https://www.usmcu.edu/Research/Marine-Corps-History-Division/People/Whos-Who-in-MarineCorps-History/Abrell-Cushman/Colonel-Barbara-Janet-Bishop/

Colonel Margaret Monroe Henderson. (n.d.). Www.usmcu.edu; United States Marine Corps University. https://www.usmcu.edu/Research/Marine-Corps-History-Division/People/Whos-Who-in-Marine-Corps-History/Gagnon-Ingram/Colonel-Margaret-MonroeHenderson/

Conductors' Strike of 1918-1919. (2021, May 20). Encyclopedia of Cleveland History | Case Western Reserve University; Case Western Reserve University. https://case.edu/ech/articles/c/conductors-strike-1918-1919

Crary, D. (2019, January 4). *Women strive for larger roles in maledominated religions.* AP NEWS; Associated Press News. https://apnews.com/article/metoo-social-media-us-news-ap-top-newsreligion-3dc6b0999bf04614b1de21863cbfdd66

Croft, R. (2018, November 7). Congresswoman Edith Nourse Rogers Tribute - VA Bedford Healthcare System. Www.bedford.va.gov; United States Department of Veteran Affairs. https://www.bedford.va.gov/

BEDFORD/features/Congresswoman_Edith_Nourse_Rogers_Tribute.asp

Cronk, T. M. (2020, October 2). *Naval Academy Was Personal Calling for First Black Female Plebe*. U.S. Department of Defense: News; United States Department of Defense. https://www.defense.gov/Explore/Features/Story/Article/2368812/naval-academy-waspersonal-calling-for-first-black-female-plebe/

Defense Now. (2021, February 5). *Annie N. Graham: First AfricanAmerican Woman to Join the Marine Corps*. Www.youtube.com. https://www.youtube.com/watch?v=tfZNmniDwMg

Eisenberg, B., & Ruthsdotter, M. (1998). History of the Women's Rights Movement | National Women's History Alliance. National Women's History Alliance. https://nationalwomenshistoryalliance.org/history-of-the-womens-rights-movement/

Equal Rights Amendment – Alice Paul Institute. (n.d.). Www.alicepaul.org; Alice Paul Institute. https://www.alicepaul.org/equalrights-amendment-2/

The Equal Rights Amendment | DPLA. (2016). Dp.la; Digital Public Library of America. https://dp.la/primary-source-sets/theequal-rights-amendment

Ermey, L. (2013). *Gunny's Rules: How to Get Squared Away Like A Marine*. Regnery Publishing, Inc. Evans, F. (2020, November 5). *Why Harry Truman ended segregation in the US Military in 1948*. HISTORY; The HISTORY Channel. https://www.history.com/news/harry-truman-executive-order9981-desegration-military-1948

Gebicke, M. E. (1993, June) GAO Report to the Secretary of Defense. In *gao.gov*. The United States General Accounting Office. https://www.gao.gov/assets/160/153531.pdf

Grady, C. (2018, March 20). *The Waves of Feminism, and Why People Keep Fighting Over Them, Explained*. Vox; Vox Media. https://www.vox.com/2018/3/20/16955588/feminism-waves-explained-firstsecond-third-fourth

Grove, D. (2018, June 18). *6 Tips for Getting Through the "Crucible" — the Final, Grueling Step in Marine Recruits' Training*. Business Insider. https://www.businessinsider.com/6-tips-for-the-cruciblethe-final-part-of-marine-recruits-training-2018-6#1-work-asa-team-1

Harper, B. (2011, July 5). Lucille Ellen McClarren The FIRST oman Marine 1943. Women Marines Association. https://womenmarines.wordpress.com/2011/07/05/lucille-ellen-mcclarren-the-firstwoman-marine-1943/

Harris, M., & Meier, S. (2018, July 26). *Crossing Milestones for Female Marines: Examining the Maria C. Villescas Collection | Folklife Today*. Blogs.loc.gov; Folklife Today: American Folklore Center and Veterans History Project, Library of Congress. https://blogs.loc.gov/folklife/2018/07/crossing-milestones-for-female-marinesexamining-the-maria-c-villescas-collection/

Helen Magill White | American educator. (n.d.). Encyclopedia Britannica; Encyclopædia Britannica, Inc. https://www.britannica.com/biography/Helen-Magill-White

History. (n.d.). YWCA Seattle | King | Snohomish; The Young Women's Club of America, Seattle, Washington. Retrieved June 27, 2021, from https://www.ywcaworks.org/history

History.com Editors. (2011, August 7). *Women in the Vietnam War*. HISTORY; The HISTORY Channel, A&E Television Networks. https://www.history.com/topics/vietnam-war/women-in-thevietnam-war#section_2

History.com Editors. (2018a, November 11). *Korean War*. HISTORY.com; The HISTORY Channel, A&E Television Networks. https://www.history.com/topics/korea/korean-war

History.com Editors. (2018, November 11). *Vietnam War Timeline*. HISTORY; The HISTORY Channel, A&E Television Networks. https://www.history.com/topics/vietnam-war/vietnam-wartimeline

History.com Editors. (2019, February 26). *Women's History Milestones: A Timeline*. HISTORY; The HISTORY Channel, A&E Television Networks. https://www.history.com/topics/womens-history/womens-history-us-timeline

Katherine Amelia Towle. (n.d.). Wikipedia. https://en.wikipedia.org/wiki/Katherine_Amelia_Towle

Katherine Amelia Towle, Colonel, U.S. Marine Corps. (2020, March 27). Foundation for Women Warriors; Foundation for Women Warriors. https://foundationforwomenwarriors.org/katherineamelia-towle-colonel-u-s-marine-corps/

Katherine Towle | 150 Years of Women at Berkeley. (n.d.). 150w.berkeley.edu; University of California, Berkeley. Retrieved June 25, 2021, from https://150w.berkeley.edu/katherine-towle

Klein, C. (2020, August 11). *5 Events That Led to the End of World War II*. HISTORY; The HISTORY Channel. https://www.history.com/news/world-war-ii-end-events

Kratz, J. A. (2017, November 9). *Vietnam and the Women Who Served – Pieces of History*. U.S. National Archives: Pieces of History; U.S. National Archives. https://prologue.blogs.archives.gov/2017/11/09/vietnam-and-the-women-who-served/

Lange, A. (2016, August 23). *History of U.S. Woman's Suffrage*. History of U.S. Woman's Suffrage; Crusade for the Vote, National Women's History Museum. http://www.crusadeforthevote.org/19-amendment/

Library of Congress. (2015). *Today in History - July 19*. The Library of Congress; U.S Library of Congress. https://www.loc.gov/item/today-in-history/july-19

Library of Congress, & Stanton, E. C. (1848). "Declaration of Sentiments." The Library of Congress; Manuscript Division, U.S. Library of Congress. https://www.loc.gov/exhibitions/womenfight-for-the-vote/about-this-exhibition/seneca-falls-and-buildinga-movement-1776-1890/seneca-falls-and-the-start-of-annualconventions/declaration-of-sentiments/

Library of Congress. *Women of Protest: Photographs from the Records of the National Woman's Party*. (2015). The Library of Congress; U.S. Library of Congress. https://www.loc.gov/collections/women-ofprotest/articles-and-essays/selected-leaders-of-the-nationalwomans-party/visionaries/

Lorenz, L. (2020, October 19). *Highlighting Our Heroes: Barbara J. Dulinsky*. Navy League of the United States; Navy League of the United States. https://www.navyleague.org/news/highlighting-ourheroes-barbara-j-dulinsky/

Makers: Women in War. (2014, October 21). Www.pbs.org; Public Broadcasting Service. https://www.pbs.org/show/makers-womenwho-make-america/

Margaret A. Brewer. (2007). Wikipedia. https://en.wikipedia.org/wiki/Margaret_A._Brewer

Marine Corps University—Colonel Ruth Cheney Streeter. (n.d.).

Www.usmcu.edu; United States Marine Corps University. https://www.usmcu.edu/Research/Marine-Corps-History-Division/People/Whos-Who-in-Marine-Corps-History/Scannell-Upshur/Colonel-Ruth-Cheney-Streeter/

Marine Time Machine: Master Sergeant Barbara Dulinsky. (2018). [Website Video]. In *United States Marine Corps*. https://www.marines.mil/News/Marines-TV/videoid/589970/

McDermott, A. (2018, September 1). Did Franz Ferdinand's Assassination Cause World War I? History.com; History, A&E Television Networks, LLC. https://www.history.com/news/did-franzferdinands-assassination-cause-world-war-i

Medgar Evers | NAACP. (n.d.). Naacp.org; National Association for the Advancement of Colored People. https://naacp.org/findresources/history-explained/civil-rights-leaders/medgar-evers

Michals, D. (2015). Alice Paul. National Women's History Museum; National Women's History Museum. https://www.womenshistory.org/education-resources/biographies/alice-paul

Michals, D. (2017). Margaret Sanger. National Women's History Museum; National Women's History Museum. https://www.womenshistory.org/education-resources/biographies/margaretsanger

Michigan Military and Veterans Hall of Honor | Margaret A. Brewer. (n.d.). Www.mimilitaryvethallofhonor.org; Michigan Military and Veterans Hall of Honor. https://www.mimilitaryvethallofhonor.org/2019/brewer.html

Mitchell, D. (2020, March 4). *Semper Fi: Kokomo native was first female Marine*. The Indianapolis Star; The Indianapolis Star. https://www.indystar.com/story/news/history/retroindy/2020/03/04/opha-johnson-kokomo-native-first-female-marine-corpshoosier/4902257002/

Molnar, Jr., A. (n.d.). *Women Marines in World War II*. Www.usmcu.edu; United States Marine Corps University. https://www.usmcu.edu/Research/Marine-Corps-History-Division/BriefHistories/Marines-in-World-War-II/Women-Marines-inWorld-War-II/

Morden, B. J. (1990). *The Women's Army Corps, 1945-1978*. Webdoc.sub.gwdg.de; Center for Military History. My Book

More Women's Rights Conventions - Women's Rights National Historical Park (U.S. National Park Service). (2015, February 26). Nps.gov; National

Park Service. https://www.nps.gov/wori/learn/historyculture/more-womens-rights-conventions.htm

Moreno, E. (2016, June). Major General Angela Salinas. *San Antonio Magazine*. https://www.sanantoniomag.com/major-general-angelasalinas/

National Archives. (n.d.). *Esther Peterson Personal Papers | JFK Library*. Www.jfklibrary.org; John F. Kennedy Presidential Library and Museum. Retrieved June 27, 2021, from https://www.jfklibrary.org/asset-viewer/archives/EEPPP

National Museum of the Marine Corps. (n.d.). Women Marine Milestones. In United States Marine Corps Museum. National Museum of the Marines Corps. https://www.usmcmuseum.com/uploads/6/0/3/6/60364049/womenmarineresources.pdf

National Park Service. (2015, February). *Declaration of Sentiments Women's Rights National Historical Park* (U.S. National Park Service). Nps.gov; U.S. National Park Service. https://www.nps.gov/wori/learn/historyculture/declaration-of-sentiments.htm

National Park Service. (2018). *Women in World War I* (U.S. National Park Service). Nps.gov. https://www.nps.gov/articles/women-inworld-war-i.htm

O'Conner, B. (2020, May 27). *Forty Years Have Passed Since the First Women Graduated from West Point in the Class of 1980*. Www.army.mil; United States Army. https://www.army.mil/article/235994/forty_years_have_passed_since_the_first_women_graduated_from_west_point_in_the_class_of_1980

Our Documents, United States Government. (2015). Our Documents - 19th Amendment to the U.S. Constitution: Women's Right to Vote (1920). Ourdocuments.gov; United States Government. https://www.ourdocuments.gov/doc.php?flash=false&doc=63

Planned Parenthood Action Fund. (2014). Plannedparenthoodaction.org; Planned Parenthood Action Fund. https://www.plannedparenthoodaction.org/issues/birth-control/burwell-vhobby-lobby

The Proceedings of the Woman's Rights Convention, Held At Worcester, October 23d & 24th, 1850. (n.d.). United States Library of Congress; United

States Library of Congress, Washington, D.C. https://www.loc.gov/resource/rbnawsa.n8286/?st=gallery

Pruitt, S. (2019, March 4). The Night of Terror: When Suffragists Were Imprisoned and Tortured in 1917. HISTORY; HISTORY Channel. https://www.history.com/news/night-terror-brutalitysuffragists-19th-amendment

Public Law 94—106. (1975, October 7). United States Congress; 94th U.S. Congress. https://www.congress.gov/94/statute/STATUTE-89/STATUTE-89-Pg531.pdf

Robinette, D. (2019, January 10). *From Quantico to Cookies: Major General Angie Salinas.* San Antonio Woman Magazine; San Antonino Woman Magazine. https://sawoman.com/2019/01/fromquantico-to-cookies-major-general-angie-salinas/

Ruth C. Streeter, 94, Ex-Leader Of Women Reserves in Marines. (1990, October 2). *The New York Times.* https://www.nytimes.com/1990/10/02/obituaries/ruth-c-streeter-94-ex-leader-of-womenreserves-in-marines.html

Ruth Cheney Streeter. (n.d.). Wikipedia. https://en.wikipedia.org/wiki/Ruth_Cheney_Streeter

Ruth Cheney Streeter, Colonel, U.S. Marine Corps. (2020, March 9). Foundation for Women Warriors; Foundation for Women Warriors. https://foundationforwomenwarriors.org/ruth-cheneystreeter-colonel-u-s-marine-corps/

Sandstrom, A. (2016, March 2). *Women relatively rare in top positions of religious leadership.* Pew Research Center; Pew Research Center. https://www.pewresearch.org/fact-tank/2016/03/02/womenrelatively-rare-in-top-positions-of-religious-leadership/

SCPR. (2014, October 21). *Retired Major General Angela Salinas Helped Blaze Trail for Women in Military.* Southern California Public Radio; Southern California Public Radio, Take Two. https://www.scpr.org/programs/take-two/2014/10/21/39917/makers-retiredmajor-general-angela-salinas-helped/

Simmons, M. Sgt. A. (2018, September 6). Opha May Johnson Memorial Unveiling. Www.marineband.marines.mil; United States Marine Corps.

https://www.marineband.marines.mil/Photos/igphoto/2001962420/

Spring, K. A. (2019). Oveta Culp Hobby. National Women's History Museum; National Women's History Museum. https://www.womenshistory.org/education-resources/biographies/oveta-hobby

Stanton, E. C. (1898). Eighty Years And More: Reminiscences 18151897 (pp. 143–144). T. Fisher Unwin. https://digital.library.upenn.edu/women/stanton/years/years.html

Stevens, D. (1920). Jailed for Freedom. In Google Books (pp. 91–145). Liveright. My Book

Straughn, G. (n.d.). *Fighting for Healthy Women and Families.* Women & the American Story; New York Historical Society Museum and Library. https://wams.nyhistory.org/modernizingamerica/fighting-for-social-reform/fighting-for-healthy-womenand-families/

Stremlow, C. M. V. (1986). *A History of the Women Marines: 1946-1947* (pp. 1–2, 18-22). History And Museums Division, Headquarters, U.S. Marine Corps. https://www.marines.mil/Portals/1/Publications/A%20History%20of%20the%20Women%20Marines%201946-1977%20PCN%202019000309400_1.pdf

Time, INC. (Ed.). (1944, March 27). Woman Marines. LIFE, 81. Google Books. http://books.google.com/books?

Toler, P. D. (2019, February 26). Not Every Woman Who Served With the U.S. Military During World War I Got the Same Treatment. Here's Why. Time Magazine; Time USA, LLC. https://time.com/5537784/wwi-us-military-women/

Trotta, D. (2021, April 26). Breaking a barrier, women become U.S. Marines after surviving the "crucible." Reuters. https://www.reuters.com/world/us/breaking-barrier-women-become-usmarines-after-surviving-crucible-2021-04-26/

United States Army. (n.d.). Regimental Command Sergeant Major-Previous Quartermaster Commandants. Quartermaster.army.mil; United States Army. https://quartermaster.army.mil/bios/previousqm-generals/previous-qm-commadants-bios.html

United States Army. (2016). Women in the United States Army, World War I (1917-1918). Army.mil; United States Army. https://www.army.mil/women/history/

United States Army. (2016). Women in the United States Army—

Creation of the Women's Army Corps. Army.mil; United States Army. https://www.army.mil/women/history/

United States Census Bureau. (2019, August 27). Signatures to the "Declaration of Sentiments." The United States Census Bureau; Library of Congress. https://www.census.gov/programs-surveys/sis/resources/historical-documents/declaration-sentiments.html

The United States of America Vietnam War Commemoration. (2020, March 13). *Women Veterans Share Their Experiences During the Vietnam War*. Www.youtube.com; The United States of America Vietnam War Commemoration. https://www.youtube.com/watch?v=NhdKObnSSmk

United States House of Representatives. (2007). The Women's Rights Movement, 1848–1917. History, Art & Archives, U.S. House of Representatives, Office of the Historian, Women in Congress, 1917–2006; U.S. Government Printing Office. https://history.house.gov/Exhibitions-and-Publications/WIC/Historical-Essays/No-Lady/Womens-Rights/

Wagner, E. (n.d.). Occoquan Workhouse (U.S. National Park Service). Www.nps.gov; National Park Service, Cultural Resources Office of Interpretation and Education. https://www.nps.gov/places/occoquan-workhouse.htm

The Washington Times. (1895, June 5). Chronicling America: Historic American Newspapers. Library of Congress. https://chroniclingamerica.loc.gov/lccn/sn87062244/1895-06-05/ed-1/seq-4/

Waxman, O. B. (2018, August 13). The First Woman Was Sworn Into the Marine Corps a Century Ago. Now a Group of Veterans Is Trying to Preserve Her Story. Time; Time Magazine. https://time.com/5363318/first-woman-marine-corps/

Wexler, C. V. (2020, January 21). *Pope Francis put a woman in a top Vatican role. It shows how little power Catholic women hold*. NBC News: Thought Experiment; NBC News. https://www.nbcnews.com/think/opinion/pope-francis-put-woman-top-vatican-role-itshows-how-ncna1119661

The Women's Armed Services Integration Act. (2019). U.S. Capitol Visitor Center; The U.S. Capitol Visitor Center. https://www.visitthecapitol.gov/exhibitions/congress-and-world-wars-part-2/womens-armed-services-integration-act

Women Marines Association. (2012). *Women Marines History: History of Women in the Marines.* Womenmarines.org; Women Marines Association. https://www.womenmarines.org/wm-history

Women Marines in the 1980's. (1986). United States Marine Corps; Division of Public Affairs, Headquarters, United States Marine Corps. https://www.marines.mil/Portals/1/Publications/Women%20Marines%20in%20the%201980's.pdf

A NOTE FROM THE AUTHOR

I do hope you have enjoyed reading this fascinating book as much as I enjoyed researching and writing it. What now you say........I invite you to take action as you continue the legacy of the women of the marines.

Click the link to download a FREE resources information booklet – Surviving and Thriving in the Marines
   www.womeninthemarines.com

My passion has been researching and writing this book for you to enjoy and I sincerely hope you did. If the book was of interest and enjoyable for you to read, I would respectfully request that you leave a positive review. This will support me in getting my book to a wider audience. I have included various links below depending upon where in the world you are based.

Thank you for reading.
   Amazon.com review link. https://amzn.to/3DCnMJZ
   Amazon.com.au link. https://amzn.to/3kR3tkA
   Amazon.co.uk link. https://amzn.to/3CE7JKq

ABOUT THE AUTHOR

Savannah Harris is a gender historian who specializes in social history and women's history. Harris plans to publish a series of books about several "Women's Firsts," and *The History of Women in the Marines* is its first volume. By publishing books on these crucial topics, she hopes to contribute to the Women's Rights Movement through her work popularizing history and presenting the lives and stories of strong women.

Harris has devoted years to researching women's rights and women's history to present the reader with a book that is both as engaging, boundary-breaking, informative, and inspiring as the women who grace its pages. This book is the product of her passion for women's independence and equality and a recognition of their rightful place in history, where they have historically been overlooked.

www.ingramcontent.com/pod-product-compliance
Lightning Source LLC
Chambersburg PA
CBHW072102110526
44590CB00018B/3278